Freemasonry in the Wild West

Freemasonry
in the
Wild West

Kyle A. Grafstrom

Plumbstone
WASHINGTON, D.C.
2017

This book has been made possible by the generous support
of Washington Masonic Charities.

Cover art: James Everett Stuart, *Sunset Glow–Mount Rainier*. Oil on canvas, 1889.
Courtesy of the Washington State Historical Society. The early seal of the Grand
Lodge of Masons of the Washington Territory is featured by special permission
of the Most Worshipful Grand Lodge, F. &A.M., of Washington.

Publisher's Cataloging-in-Publication data
Grafstrom, Kyle A., 1983–
    Freemasonry in the wild west / Kyle A. Grafstrom
    224 p.   27 cm.
    ISBN-13   978-1-60302-026-8 (hardcover)
    ISBN-13   978-1-60302-027-5 (paperback)
    1. Freemasonry—History. 2. Freemasons. 3. West (U.S.)—History.
    4. Astoria (Or.)—History. 5. Frontier and pioneer life—West (U.S.)
    I. Title.
    SOCIAL SCIENCE / Freemasonry & Secret Societies.
    HISTORY / United States / State & Local / West (AK, CA, CO, HI, ID,
       MT, NV, UT, WY).
    HISTORY / United States / State & Local / Pacific Northwest (OR, WA).
    HS414.G73 2017   366´.1—dc23.

Library of Congress Control Number: 2017963023

http://www.plumbstone.com

To my parents, Timothy and Melodie Grafstrom.

Contents

Foreword

FOR MANY AMERICANS, the term "Wild West" evokes the classic romantic fantasies of cowboys and Indians, vast prairies, foreboding sierras, gold and silver rushes, and a lawless, unforgiving environment. These images are largely perpetuated by movies, television shows, and, of course, the requisite elementary school lessons. For those of us who grew up in the West, the latter was accentuated by a trip to a ghost town where we were taught to pan for gold, ride a horse, and perhaps don a generic misshapen cowboy hat. And whereas most of us now recognize the terror that befell the original Native American tribes, most do not fully understand the territory itself, nor the other people who first arrived following the original conquest of the Americas in 1492: there were the Spanish, who, by 1821, were considered Mexican subjects without doing anything themselves; the French; the Russians, the British, and finally the Americans.

These histories are highly complex, transcending discussions of heroic names and pivotal battles. There are entire centuries to be remembered and studied. We can certainly write tomes about the horrors of the conquest and about how the culture of the invaders altered and destroyed those of the natives. This is historic record, and nothing can change the facts.

During the first quarter of the nineteenth century, the West was still a wilderness of dangerous and foreboding terrain, but those who traveled there were no longer conquerors. Today we simply call them pioneers, but much of the danger and loneliness that was a daily reality to them has been lost to us. With a full understanding of what these people experienced, we'd prefer to call them "extreme" adventurers, or even plain crazy.

Then there were the regions that even the Native Americans didn't even go; places known to be certain death. These were Nature's kingdoms, not men's. In fact, this was a territory were one could die with no name and never be buried, and the family would wait for decades, painfully wondering if a letter from him would arrive that day, or the next. Weeks would pass into months into years. What happened to him? Did he die frozen and alone? Perhaps he was killed by natives? Perhaps by a wild beast… or perhaps by his own friend?

Fraternal orders such as Freemasonry have long promised and provided socio-cultural cohesion and protection for their members. At any point in history for imperial societies, be they armies or intrepid bands of pioneers, these qualities have taken on a very real meaning. For those who traveled West, their fraternal bonds brought together like minds at the least, and the best minds and brawn at the most. As the Americans spread west, the rule of New Spain was in its nadir, and Mexico was to ascend. Still, it was a large territory, and the power of men could never conquer such a large land. During the period of 1810-1848, these men (and they were mostly men) were able to carve out a place in a region of growing dispute over who controlled what. They would set up trapping industries to compete with the formidable Hudson's Bay Company; they would arrive in peace and be content to marry into existing families and inherit vast ranchos and orchards; and like their not-too-distant colonial countrymen, they would foment discord against a foreign government. And by 1848, they would watch western gates open to a river of gold, and the rest of the world would conquer even their own.

Kyle Grafstrom's narrative guides us back to the decades prior to the gold rush, beyond the well-told tale of Lewis and Clark, to the remote hinterlands where trails were not yet cut and fur trappers became successful barons, or reduced to cutthroat tactics. From soldiers of fortune to mountain men, and to farmers seeking out wealthy Spanish families in order to obtain more land that he could dream—to tribal warfare, wrecked wagon trains, and anonymous grave markers dotting the landscape, this is a tale of the American journey West and the fraternity that caused true friendship to exist "among those who might have otherwise remained at a perpetual distance."

Adam Kendall
Editor, *The Plumbline*, Scottish Rite Research Society
Past Curator, The Henry W. Coil Library
& Museum of Freemasonry

Preface

VERY FEW ORGANIZATIONS can compare to the history of the Freemasons. Boasting an all star cast of the 'who's who' of men that changed the world, it is no wonder Freemasonry captivates the mind of most anyone who hears about it. Thoughts of what could lie beyond the veil of "secrets" lead people to all manner of wild ideas. The most common refrain of the critic of Freemasonry is that some foul play or corrupt activity must be the reason for the ancient society's insistence upon privacy. But it is a staggering prospect to imagine men such as Theodore Roosevelt, Benjamin Franklin, Amadeus Mozart, and Winston Churchill, meeting behind closed doors for dishonorable purposes. And, certainly, these men are just a few threads in the immense tapestry interwoven by the lives of extraordinary men who all just "happened" to be Masons.

The question is not "What did Freemasonry do for these men?" but rather, "Why did they do what they did for Freemasonry?" That answer is of course left to interpretation. The fact which shall soon be made apparent to you in this reading, is that many of the men who pioneered the west were Freemasons.

I know that in my own experience, it has always been inspiration that has pushed me forward in this fraternity. It is without a doubt the role models I have found in Freemasonry both in person and in print that have led me to think as highly of the Craft as I do.

My intention with sharing this rich stretch of history is to bring to light the riches that are at our feet every time we step into a Masonic lodge. I hope that as a result of reading the reader will come to find a greater appreciation for just how important Freemasonry was to these honorable brothers of the past and consequently be inspired to do more today.

Kyle Grafstrom
Verity Lodge № 59
Kent, Washington

CAPITOL CORNERSTONE CEREMONY · 1793

INTRODUCTION

> Every man needs a picture, or metaphor,
> of what he is doing and what it means to
> be a man. Our role as American men is to
> maintain the stability of our country. It is up
> to us to stay the course of what constitutes
> the best ideals in masculinity.
> —Brother Robert Davis[1]

ON SEPTEMBER 18TH, 1793, President George Washington laid the cornerstone of the United States Capitol Building in one of the most public and well known Masonic events in American history. This solemn ceremony perfectly embodied the shared ideals of both the American Republic and the Masonic fraternity. By honoring civic virtues, liberty and the Supreme Architect, a new era of governance was ushered in by the first Freemason-President.

George Washington was obviously more than a man, more than a Freemason, and more than our first President. He was the archetypal Father destined to raise our country from its infancy. His name and face are literally synonymous with America. As a result of this, when Washington appeared publicly in his Masonic apron on that crisp fall day, he forever linked Freemasonry with high office in the United States. In the years that followed, countless similar public Masonic events caused the fraternity "to be seen as a key element in attempts to spread liberty and create public virtue."[2]

In the two hundred and twenty plus years since the dedication of the Capital Building, our country has undergone enormous changes. We have fluctuated between great economic booms and terrible depressions.

---

1   Robert G. Davis, *Understanding Manhood in America: Freemasonry's Enduring Path to the Mature Masculine* (Richmond, Va.: Anchor Communications, 2005), 15.

2   Steven Bullock, *Revolutionary Brotherhood: Freemasonry and the Transformation of the American Social Order, 1730–1840* (Chapel Hill, N.C.: University of North Carolina Press. 1996), 4.

Politically, the pendulum has swung back and forth as the demands of the people have constantly shifted. Culturally, we have only grown more diverse as the years have passed. Despite everything that has happened, the great American experiment lives on.

Considering the turmoil in which our nation often found itself in years immediately after Brother Washington's passing in 1799, it is remarkable that the United States was able to survive. The country initially grew at an explosive rate that could hardly be imagined today. Every decade the U.S. population grew by an average of 30%.[3] Imagine if the town you live in grew by 30% every ten years. How difficult would it be to preserve tradition let alone law and order?

Needless to say, the 1800s were a tumultuous and exciting time to be alive, especially for young men. "Seldom has there been a time so favorable to men who were strong in character as well as instincts. To the people of a young and rapidly expanding nation, a single venture often appeared to enclose both the interests of the nation and the interests of the entrepreneur."[4] During this period of wild expansion in the U.S., there also occurred a curious growth among the Masonic fraternity. Seemingly without exception, Masonic lodges were almost always one of the first buildings of a new town and moreover the settlers and founders of towns were often Masons. This correlation is not brought up to suggest a cause and effect but rather to highlight the constant presence of Freemasons in the American narrative.

Since time immemorial, the benevolent society of Freemasonry has existed with the purpose of bringing together good men for moral and philosophical improvement. In addition to teaching men to be better, Freemasonry provides them with an organizing principle that allows for truly universal fellowship.[5] It is no wonder that Freemasonry spread so quickly during the early years of the United States.

Just like they had become so popular during the social chaos of early eighteenth-century London, American Masonic Lodges would help fill the social vacuum for men in cities across the United States. After becom-

3   Official U.S. Census data. *https://www.census.gov/population/www/censusdata/hiscendata.html.*

4   Robert Stuart *&* Kenneth A. Spaulding, *On the Oregon Trail: Robert Stuart's Journey of Discovery* (Ann Arbor, Mi.: UMI, 1991).

5   One of the oldest Masonic documents, Anderson's *Constitutions*, states in the first charge that "Masonry becomes the Center of Union, and the Means of conciliating true Friendship among Persons that must else have remain'd at a perpetual distance."

ing a Mason, a man could travel virtually anywhere and tap into a social network in the new city.

> The rise of Ancient Masonry and the resolution of wartime troubles launched the fraternity into a period of unparalleled growth. Within a generation after the Revolution, American Masonry grew from a few scattered groups of brothers to a well-organized and pervasive organization gathering in nearly every locality in America. Indeed, more lodges met in the United States in 1825 than in the entire world fifty years before.[6]

Thanks to their influence on both the individual and society overall, Masonic lodges were established in nearly every major city in the United States. As major cities burst at the seams and the country expanded westward, Freemasonry followed suit bringing with it a highly beneficial social and philosophical system.

In this book, the reader will take a journey back into the the birth of the Wild West, tracing the development of the first half of the nineteenth century and the influence that Freemasons had during the time period. While the work put in to produce this story has been substantial, the author believes he has only scratched the surface and hopes there will be others who will be able to dig deeper.

---

6   Bullock, *Revolutionary Brotherhood*, 138.

1810 *to* 1813

John Jacob Astor
and
His Fur Empire

No MASONIC HISTORY of the West would be complete without acknowledging the three Masonic Goliaths that left their mark on the region in the first decade of the nineteenth century. Two were Meriwether Lewis and William Clark, who led the famous journey in 1804 beyond the Rockies to find a suitable route from St Louis to the Pacific.[1] This tale about two young and adventurous Freemasons is already well known so it will not be retold here. The third and lesser known Mason to influence the West was brother John Jacob Astor just a few years later in 1811. His business interests and financial power led to the first American settlement on the West Coast, the Pacific equivalent of Jamestown.[2] This incredible venture would prove to be just the first move in a decades long chess match to claim the Pacific Northwest.

Brother John Jacob Astor
Holland Lodge No. 8, New York City in 1788

"Your name will be handed down with that of Columbus…as the father of the establishment and the founder of such an empire."
Thomas Jefferson to John Jacob Astor[3]

At the ripe age of sixteen, Astor left his hometown village of Walldorf, Germany to work with his older brother in England making musical instruments. There the young visionary looked beyond his surroundings and dreamed of a life in America. It only took him four years to earn enough to buy a ticket across the Atlantic, which he did in 1784.

He arrived in Chesapeake Bay at the age of twenty-one.[4] He then made his way to New York City, where he entered the capital of the six-year-old United States. Our fledgling nation was just beginning to spread its wings and would soon nearly double in size due to the Louisiana Purchase.

1   William Clark was made a Mason at St. Louis Lodge N⁰ 111 in Missouri, and Meriwether Lewis made a Mason at Door to Virtue Lodge N⁰ 44 in Albermarle County, Virginia, and later the first Master of St. Louis Lodge N⁰ 111 in 1808 where Clark joined. *http://stlmasons.org/history.*

2   Peter Stark, *Astoria: John Jacob Astor and Thomas Jefferson's Lost Pacific Empire* (New York: HarperCollins, 2014), 2.

3   "Your name will be handed down with that of Columbus & Raleigh"—Thomas Jefferson to John Jacob Astor, November 9, 1813, in *The Papers of Thomas Jefferson* (Princeton, N.J.: Princeton University Press), 6:603.

4   Stark, *Astoria*, 1:11.

John Wesley Jarvis (1780–1840), *John Jacob Astor.*
Oil on canvas, c. 1825. National Portrait Gallery, Washington, D.C.

It can be assumed that pretty much everyone in New York city at the time had come to America looking for a better life. John Jacob wasted no time doing this and eventually became involved in exporting luxurious furs to Europe.

At the time, what Astor was doing was nothing new, he just had a bigger vision than the average merchant. Indeed, his rags to riches story would become the epitome of the American Dream in later years. With his business interests eventually encompassing China, North America and Europe, he went on to become the richest man in the world during his

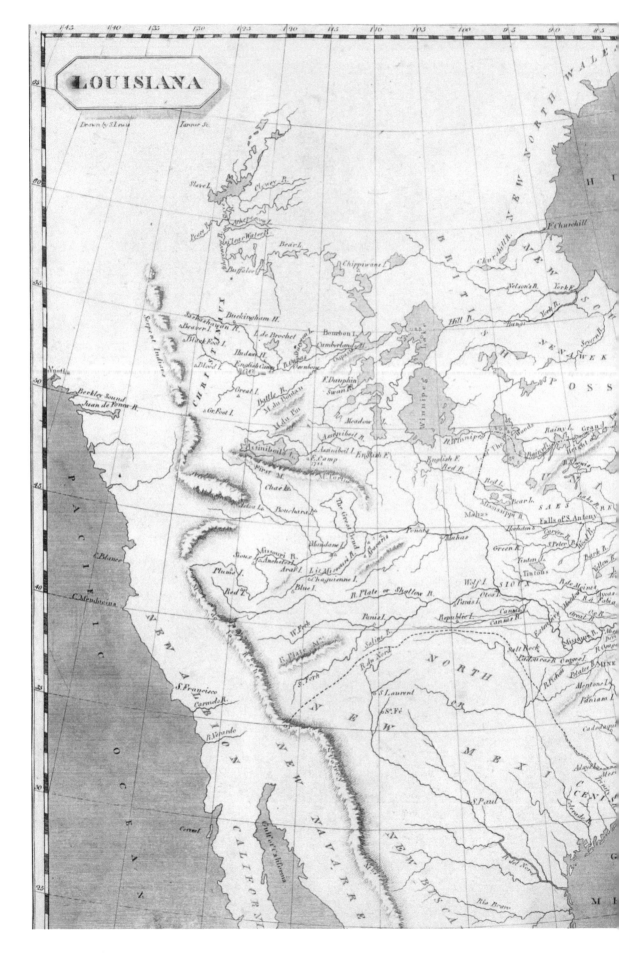

LOUISIANA

Drawn by S. Lewis   Tanner Sc.

lifetime.[5]

One of Astor's earliest business partnerships was with Indian Fur traders of the Great Lakes region. This made sense as it afforded him direct access to the precious furs with no middle men. At first, he personally went out and did the trading but as his business grew he spent more time managing his affairs in New York City. Before long he had a steady supply of furs he was able to acquire for pennies on the dollar which he then resold for huge profits overseas. Possessed with pure entrepreneurial spirit, his business continued to grow and eventually he chartered it under the "American Fur Company." Then, something happened that shook not only the fur industry, but also the entire psyche of America.

In 1806, Meriwether Lewis and William Clark returned to the United States from a successful journey to the Pacific Coast. This event transformed the American sensibility, proving once and for all that western expansion was possible. Perhaps more importantly, it also demonstrated that a direct route to the Chinese market could be established as an alternative to sailing around the Cape of South America.[6]

The Louisiana Purchase

The dawn of the nineteenth century in the United States was truly like no other time in the history of our country. Through tremendous hardship the United States had emerged victorious after the Revolutionary War. Now an independent nation of endless opportunity, we were attracting immigrants at a rate that can hardly be imagined today. In 1800, the U.S. census accounted for a little over five million American residents. Ten years later that number had ballooned by 35% to over seven million residents.[7] These new American citizens would need jobs, places to live, and food.

Fortunately for the country, there was a brilliant man destined to lead it through the chaos. That man was Thomas Jefferson, who came into the presidential office in 1800. At stake during his presidency was the entire American democracy and to his genius we as a nation owe many things.

---

5   *http://www.forbes.com/2007/09/14/richest-americans-alltime-biz_cx_pw_as_0914all-time_slide_5.html?thisSpeed=30000.*

6   China was at the time in the greatest demand for furs of all markets and traded valuable silks, teas and other "exotic" goods which were in turn sold at huge profits in American markets.

7   *https://www.census.gov/history/www/through_the_decades/fast_facts/1800_fast_facts.html.*

One of the most important contributions attributed to Jefferson was the Louisiana Purchase. Through this deal the United States was assured plenty of room to grow.

This vast and relatively unknown region that lay west of the Mississippi, the Louisiana Territory, had already exchanged hands several times prior to 1800. It had already been claimed by the Spanish, the French and the indigenous Mississippian culture which originally claimed the region prior to Spanish arrival in the 1500s.[8] In 1803 the region changed hands for the final time, from the French to the United States through the Louisiana Purchase.[9]

Jefferson wasted no time after the U.S. acquired the Louisiana Territory before he dispatched the Lewis and Clark Corps of Discovery. But contrary to popular American mythos, this would not be the first time a group of white men crossed the North American continent by land. In 1793, a Scottish born explorer named Alexander Mackenzie successfully completed the first ever (recorded) transcontinental crossing of North America, beating Lewis and Clark by twelve years.[10] When reports of this expedition were published in 1801, Jefferson knew he had to make a move for the Pacific Northwest. He could not allow the British to gain control of the region and so the Corps of Discovery set out to determine the best course to reach it. Five years later, Jefferson completed this objective and in effect created a blueprint for Astor to reach the west coast.

John Jacob Astor was, by this time (1806), an established and powerful merchant in New York City, and his American Fur Company was just one of several spreading its tentacles westward in search of furs. The prized possession for all fur companies was to be the first to establish a trading post on the Columbia River and thus control this hub of the Western coast. Astor wrote to Jefferson petitioning him to sponsor his companies journey to establish such a post however Astor

8   The Mississippian culture was a mound-building Native American civilization that flourished in what is now the Midwestern, Eastern, and Southeastern United States from 800 to 1600.

9   James Monroe and (Brother) Robert R. Livingston had traveled to Paris to negotiate the purchase of New Orleans in January 1803. Their instructions were to negotiate or purchase control of New Orleans and its environs; they did not anticipate the much larger acquisition which would follow. The Louisiana Purchase was by far the largest territorial gain in U.S. history. Stretching from the Mississippi River to the Rocky Mountains, the purchase doubled the size of the United States.

10   He arrived at Bella Coola, British Columbia on July 22, 1793, and unknowingly missed meeting the famed captain George Vancouver at by forty-eight days.

Brother Wilson Price Hunt (1783–1842), ca. 1840.

would have to go it alone. Fortunately for Astor, he had the capital to reach the Columbia and in his eyes the rewards far outweighed the risks of getting there.

Astor meticulously planned out the expedition for several years. He was an extremely calculated man and spared no expense in this venture. To ensure the settlement had the greatest chance of success, he chartered a new company by the name of the Pacific Fur Company which would take two different routes to the mouth of the Columbia River. One would be by land following much of the well-mapped Lewis and Clark Trail and the other by sailing around South America. The overland party would be led by brother Wilson Price Hunt, a Freemason and merchant from St. Louis while the sea route would be led by Captain Jonathan Thorn, a battle-tested Naval officer.[11]

Overland Journey to Fort Astoria: 1810

Comprising a party of approximately sixty souls, the overland journey was essentially a copy of the Lewis and Clark expedition from five years before, the main difference being that it was privately funded by one wealthy individual (rather than by Congress).[12] The group contained fifty-seven men, one Native American woman, and her two small children.

While it may have been relatively straightforward on paper for Astor to plan for the expedition, it was a different story for one of its leaders, Wilson Price Hunt, to hire a competent team. Here was one man, operating on the full faith and credit of one of the weathiest people in the world, in charge of hiring a team to trek across the wilderness in search of riches.[13] To do this, he had to recruit trappers, hunters, canoe men and clerks to willing to sign up for a three-year commitment that would take them into into a relatively unknown world.

As there was no time to sit around and wait for these people to come to him, Hunt set out on a large geographical sweep in order to find the appropriate men for the job. Accompanying Hunt on this head hunting mission was an experienced fur trader named Donald M'Kenzie. Mr. M'Kenzie had well over a decade of service with the powerful Northwest Fur Company of Canada under his belt, so he was a very competent man to have on the team.[14] The two left St. Louis and headed north to Montreal where they hoped to purchase all the equipment they needed and more importantly, find men willing to enlist with the brand new Pacific Fur Company.[15]

Hunt had at his disposal Astor's excellent credit which was eventually

---

11   T.C. Elliot, "The Earliest Travelers on the Oregon Trail." *The Quarterly of the Oregon Historical Society* 13 (March 1912), 73.

12   Letter from Thomas Jefferson to Congress, dated Jan 18, 1803, seeking $2,500 for the "purpose of extending the external commerce of the United States." Library of Congress. *https://www.monticello.org/site/jefferson/jeffersons-confidential-letter-to-congress.*

13   Hunt was known to be an upright and honest man who had been in the fur trading supplies business in St. Louis prior to this engagement. See Irving, *Astoria*, 1:179.

14   The North West Company was a fur trading business headquartered in Montreal from 1779 to 1821. It was in competition with the Hudson's Bay Company and John Jacob Astor's American Fur Company.

15   Washington Irving, *Astoria, or Anecdotes of an Enterprise Beyond the Rocky Mountains* (New York: Pollard & Moss, 1883), 1:173.

Charles Deas (1818–1867), *Voyageurs*.
Oil on canvas, 1846. Museum of Fine Arts, Boston.

carried with him all the way to Astoria. He could literally buy anything in Montreal he wanted. Not surprisingly, the boats they purchased with Astor's money were serious crafts. Measuring thirty to forty feet long and three feet wide, they were built from birch bark, sewn together with the roots of a spruce tree. The small vessels were held together with pine tar, in a manner similar to modern day kevlar and fiberglass canoes.[16] While primitive in comparison to our canoes of today, these boats could easily carry up to four tons each. In addition to the heavy cargo these canoes carried, they were the lifeboat of six to eight souls that heartily paddled inside. At the bow and stern were seated veteran paddlers, capable of steering clear of logs and rocks and as a result earned double wages for their more serious responsibilities.

It was common practice in the fur trade for men to enlist with a company for a contracted term of several years.[17] The two dominant fur trading companies were the North West Company (Scottish and French Canadians) and the Hudson's Bay company (British).

The Fur trade was the biggest economic driver of the region and one

16 Irving, *Astoria*, 1:173.

17 See Anne Farrar Hyde, *Empires, Nations and Families: A History of the North American West, 1800–1860* (Lincoln: University of Nebraska Press, 2011), 7.

Chaudiere Falls, Ottawa River, Upper Canada. 1830
Lithograph, Toronto Public Library

of the most lucrative businesses in the world at the time. It was comprised of Indian trappers (later Euro American trappers who learned the skills), merchants, clerks, bankers and politicians. The French were first to establish the trade in 1700s, but it was gradually taken over by British and American companies.

As a result of the enlistment custom in the fur trade, most of the competent men were already enlisted with one of the local fur companies. In addition to experienced trappers, Hunt and M'Kenzie needed to hire "voyageurs" who were the masters of long distance paddling.[18] Voyageurs were hard drinking, hard living laborers that were essential for a fur company in getting goods transported up and down rivers and portaged across land if needed. Unfortunately for Mr. Hunt, he was only able to hire a few unemployed voyageurs sitting about that weren't in the best condition.

July, 1810

Hunt and his nucleus of men left Montreal and paddled nearly 700 miles

18 Canadian Voyaguers were highly respected canoe men that paddled up and downriver transporting valuable cargoes of fur from forts to merchants. They often dressed in a strange combination of French jackets, scarves, and hats with Native American fringed leather pants and moccasins.

across a well established fur traders route to a large trading post between Lake Michigan and Lake Huron called Fort Michilimackinac. This location was the "great place of arrival and departure of the southwest fur trade"[19] and as a European settlement, was well over 100 years old at the time.[20] Here again, Hunt had a difficult time finding skilled voyageurs for his team. Those he did enlist had to be bought by paying off fines, bar tabs, judgements and contracts with other fur trading companies.[21]

August, 1810

A notable man enlisted at Fort Michilimackinac was Ramsay Crooks, a veteran of the North West Company[22] and familiar with the customs of Missouri River Native Americans.[23] He warned of the dangers he recently encountered with Sioux Indians and provided first hand accounts of what to expect on what would only be the first leg of their journey West. By mid August, Hunt left Fort Michilimackinac with his slightly larger crew and paddled back down to St. Louis to make his final preparations.[24]

---

19 At certain times of the year, it would be abuzz with fur traders back from their hunting/trading expeditions to liquidate their goods. See Irving, *Astoria*, 1:175.

20 French Missionary Father Jacques Marquette had established a mission on Mackinac Island in 1671, which later developed into the military Fort de Baude in 1681, and later into Fort Michilimackinac in 1715. *http://en.wikipedia.org/wiki/Mackinaw_City,_Michigan.*

21 Irving, *Astoria*, 1:179.

22 North West employees "held themselves up as the chivalry of the fur trade. They were men of iron; proof against cold weather . . . generally wore large feathers in their caps." See Irving, *Astoria*, 1:177.

23 Sioux and Blackfeet tribes who were growing more hostile with Euro-American traders.

24 It is worthy of mention to note how many miles Hunt had to travel in less than a years time to acquire all his essentials. From St. Louis to Montreal he covered 1,000 miles and from thence to Fort Michilimackinac and back to St. Louis another 1,400 miles.

Background on the Fur Industry

When Europeans began arriving in North America, the beaver was likely the most widespread and successful mammal on the continent living nearly everywhere there was sufficient water.[1] Population estimates from before the fur trading era put the intact population of wild beavers somewhere between 60 to 200 million animals across North America. Compare that number with the estimates of wild buffalo being around sixty million prior to their demise and you get a good idea how many beavers there were.

Before Europeans put a large price tag on their backs, beavers were mostly valued for their succulent meat by Native Americans and for the warmth the fur provided.[2] Their pelts were not viewed as a valuable status symbol as they later would be with European top hats, rather the Native Americans stitched the furs together into essential clothing items during the cold season.

Meanwhile across "the pond" in Europe, beaver top hats were becoming a craze in men's fashion. When these hats first became popular is not known, but we do know that the oldest reference to a beaver top hat goes back to the late fourteenth-century *Canterbury Tales*, which mentions a merchant wearing a "flandrish beaver hat."[3] The rise of the beaver hat as the status symbol for European men was not until the end of the reign of Queen Elizabeth I.[4]

At that time, high quality beaver hats were not only the most expensive hats in England but throughout all of Europe.[5] This rising demand for beaver furs led to the eventual extinction of the species throughout all of Europe and eventually Russia.[6] With no comparable alternative to beaver felt, European demand for the precious resource was strong enough that before long beaver pelts were being imported from North America.

The Dutch were the first to colonize the area which became synonomous with fur trading in North America: Hudson's Bay. Here in the early 1600s, trade relationships were established with various Native tribes creating a vast network centered around this precious commodity. There was so much money to be made in furs that in 1670, King Charles II issued a Royal Charter creating the Hudson's Bay Company. As a result, HBC held a monopoly on much of the early fur trade across North America and was at one time the largest land owner in the world.[7] It is currently the oldest continually operating company in the Western world, and it still operates a major department store chain across Canada.[8]

As trade expanded through the 1600s and early 1700s and the demand grew for fine furs in European markets, so did the demand for superior European goods by the Native Americans they traded with. Kettles, steel hatchets and knives, pots, pans, beads, blankets, firearms, ammunition, gun powder, and liquor all were extremely valuable for Natives.[9]

Eventually a global empire grew up around this industry involving American, Chinese, French and British merchants. It is hard to compare the industry to one of today when you look at the astronomical profit margins. Sea otter pelts purchased for 6 pence in the NW sold for $100 in Canton China[10] and basic furs brought in 300-500% returns and in extreme cases as much as 2,200% in returns.[11] One Boston ship in 1804 cleared $156,743 after expenses.[12]

To put these figures into a modern day perspective, consider the profits made in producing cocaine: "Processed cocaine is available in Colombia for $1500 dollars per kilo and sold on the streets of America for as much as $66,000 a kilo (a 4,300% return)."[13] This comparison between the fur trade and the illegal cocaine trade in South America goes further when one considers that both end up in the hands of mainly wealthy upper-class citizens.

Though the wilderness West of the Mississippi spanned thousands upon thousands of square miles of unexplored territory, fierce competition grew among the big fur companies who were all competing for the same limited resource.

Before long, the beaver population of Eastern North America dropped significantly. This left only one option: trappers would need to venture deeper into the Western frontier. Out of this new expansion arose many new settlements which eventually developed into prominent cities, but the most significant of the era and to the fur trade was St. Louis.

1   Eric Jay Dolin, *Fur, Fortune, and Empire: The Epic History of the Fur Trade in America* (New York: Norton, 2010), 17; Alice Outwater, Water: A Natural History (New York: BasicBooks, 1996), 21.

2   Mari Sandoz, *The Beaver Men: Spearheads of Empire* (New York: Hastings House, 1964), 46.

3   Geoffrey Chaucer, *The Canterbury Tales of Chaucer*, Edited by Thomas Tyrwhitt (Edinburgh: James Nicol, 1860). 1:9.

4   Dolin, *Fur, Fortune, and Empire*, 22.

5   John Thomson, *A Treatise on Hat-Making and Felting* (Philadelphia: H.C. Baird, 1868), 17.

6   Dolin, *Fur, Fortune, and Empire*, 22.

7   By its Royal Charter, HBC owned "Rupert's Land" which was the whole Hudson Bay drainage basin consisting of 1.5 million square miles.

8   The company is listed on the Toronto Stock Exchange under the symbol HBC.

9   Peter C. Newman, *Empire of the Bay: The Company of Adventures that Seized a Continent* (New York: Penguin Books, 1998), 164.

10 Dolin, *Fur, Fortune, and Empire*, 144.

11 Dolin, *Fur, Fortune, and Empire*, 136.

12 James R. Gibson, *Otter Skins, Boston Ships, and China Goods: The Maritime Fur Trade of the Northwest Coast, 1785–1841* (Seattle: University of Washington Press, 1992), 57.

13 *http://www.pbs.org/wgbh/pages/frontline/shows/drugs/special/math.html.*

September, 1810

Arriving back in St. Louis must have been a relief for Hunt as he now had the essential Canadian Voyageurs and experienced fur traders of the North in his crew. But there was no time to rest, he had to start up the Missouri River immediately as its upper portions (in modern day Montana) would soon freeze over and delay his departure until the Spring of 1811. With several other companies simultaneously racing to build the first fort on the Columbia, a delay of this type was not an option.

Harvey W. Johnson (1921–2005). *Keelboat on Rapids.*
Oil on canvas. Courtesy of Scott Johnson.

St. Louis

At the nucleus of the vast and cosmopolitan trade network, St. Louis sits right on the forks of two major fur trade routes: the Missouri and Mississippi Rivers. Fur trappers would depart St. Louis venturing up the Missouri River into the wilderness to hunt, trap and trade and when the season was right, return to St. Louis to sell their furs to merchants. Merchants would then load these furs onto barges destined for New Orleans, where they would be transfered to larger ships headed to New York, London and Canton.[25]

Furs were the central economic driver of the region and the industry was among the most profitable businesses in the world to be in at the time.

> All of these circumstances combined to produce a population at St. Lou-
> is even still more motley than that at Mackinaw (Michilimackinac).
> Here were to be seen, about the river banks, the hectoring, extravagant,
> bragging boatmen of the Mississippi, with the gay, grimacing, singing,
> good-humored Canadian voyageurs. Vagrant Indians, of various tribes,
> loitered about the streets. Now and then a stark Kentucky hunter, in
> leathern hunting-dress, with rifle on shoulder and knife in belt, strode

25   Hyde, *Empires, Nations and Families*, 7.

Hiram Martin Chittenden (1858–1917), Map of the Trans-Mississippi of the United States during the period of the American fur trade as conducted from St. Louis between the years 1807 and 1843. Multi-colored route added to highlight the three legs of Hunt's overland journey. Image: Library of Congress.

along. Here and there were new brick houses and shops, just set up by bustling, driving and eager men of traffic from the Atlantic States; while on the other hand, the old French mansions, with open casements, still retained the easy, indolent air of the original colonists ....[26]

October, 1810

Brother Wilson Price Hunt made his departure from St. Louis on the 21st of

26 Irving, *Astoria*, 1:186.

October, just before the onset of "winter" conditions on the Missouri River which began as early as November.[27] His group was distributed amongst three keel boats, similar to the vessels used by the Lewis and Clark journey and they would use manpower to propel themselves upriver.[28]

November, 1810

After paddling four hundred miles up the Missouri River, the group reached a place near modern day St. Joseph, Missouri. Little could anyone have known at the time that this location would in forty years be affectionately called "St. Joe" by migrants as they set off for the West. Hundreds of thousands of migrants would load their wagons and follow much of the same path Hunt was about to take. In 1810, this location was just Hunt's winter camp, chosen for its plentiful game.

January, 1811

As the group settled in for the winter, they were joined by several trappers who saw their encampment while paddling back downstream from their hunting season. These trappers provided priceless information about conditions up river. One of the reports that started to worry Hunt was that the large and powerful Sioux tribe was becoming more and more hostile with trappers. Having no one in his group that could translate or speak in the Sioux language, Hunt decided to head back to St. Louis to hire someone who could.

In January, Hunt returned to St. Louis in order to obtain a Sioux translator and more hunters.[29] The great Sioux Nation covered parts of the modern day territory of North and South Dakota, Nebraska, Wyoming and Montana. They would be the first major Native American tribe Hunt's party would encounter on the Missouri River.[30]

After a twenty-day trip back down the Missouri River, Hunt set out

27 Irving, *Astoria*, 1:188.

28 Poling, paddling and pulling by tow-line from shore or wading along the shore were the three main methods of moving upriver. Rarely were sails able to be used and steam ships did not come into use until 1819 with the ship *Indepedence*. *http://en.wikipedia.org/wiki/Missouri_River#Navigation*.

29 Irving, *Astoria*, 1:189.

30 The Sioux are a tribe comprised of three divisions: the Santee, the Yankton-Yanktonai, and the Lakota (also called the Teton). *http://en.wikipedia.org/wiki/Sioux*.

Karl Bodmer (1809–1893), *Camp Gros Ventures Of The Prairies.*
Engraving and aquatint, 1839. See *Travels in the Interior of North America*

in the streets of St. Louis to hire an interpreter.[31] Eventually he was able to hire a man by the name of Pierre Dorion, a half French-half Sioux former employee of the Missouri Fur Company.[32] He also happened to be the son of Dorian, the French translator who accompanied Merriweather Lewis and William Clark five years before in their journey to the Pacific.[33] His pay rate as hunter and interpreter was $300 a year (for the next three years) with a $200 advance for signing up.[34]

It was Pierre who ended up getting the better end of the bargain, for not only was he escaping a debt owed to the Missouri Fur Company for a large whiskey tab he had acquired, but he also demanded his wife

31 Irving, *Astoria*, 1:189.
32 The Missouri Fur Company was the major fur company in St. Louis around this time (1810). It was managed by Manuel Lisa, a Spainiard by birth and major competitior with Astor's interests in setting up posts on the Missouri and Columbia River. *http://en.wikipedia.org/wiki/Missouri_Fur_Company.*
33 Irving, *Astoria*, 1:198.
34 Irving, *Astoria*, 1:199.

and two sons accompany him on the journey as well. Hunt clearly had no other options available, and so this is how a woman and two children joined the overland party.[35] His goals met in St. Louis for the second time, Hunt set off again upriver to rejoin his original crew.

April, 1811

The party now consisted of nearly sixty persons of whom five were partners, one, John Reed, was a clerk; forty were Canadian voyageurs and the rest were hunters. They embarked in four boats, one of which was of large size, mounted with two howitzers. All were furnished with masts and sails, to be used when the wind was sufficiently favorable and strong to overpower the current of the river.

> Their encampments at night were often pleasant and picturesque…tents were pitched, fires made, meals prepared by the voyageurs, and many a story was told, and joke passed, and song sung round the evening fire. All however were asleep at an early hour.[36]

May, 1811

The overland journey had covered some 600 to 700 miles upriver by the time some members of the party got cold feet and decided to turn around and head back. Shockingly, a pair of hunters did just this and deserted the group without any provisions. This was a tough blow to the rest of the group as they were experienced riflemen who would be needed when they entered hostile territory.[37]

Fortunately, they reached a village of the Omaha tribe without any further losses and set up a camp.[38] They counted eighty tipis at this location which was only a fraction of their population just years before. The tribes recent encounter with smallpox had decimated most of the tribe in 1802.[39]

At the time of Hunt's visit, clerks noted only two hundred men, a

---

35   Irving, *Astoria*, 1:200.

36   Irving, *Astoria*, 1:219–20.

37   Irving, *Astoria*, 1:222.

38   The word Omaha (actually Umonhon or Umanhan) means "Dwellers on the bluff." See J.J. Mathews, *The Osages: Children of the Middle Waters* (Norman, Okla.: University of Oklahoma Press, 1961), 110.

39   *http://www.neh.gov/humanities/2002/novemberdecember/feature/ancestral-bones.*

drastic drop from the powerful tribe estimated to be 4,000 in number a century before.[40]

They camped with this tribe for a few days, but before long Mr. Hunt grew anxious at the rumors circulating about the neighboring Sioux tribe. Towards the middle of May they left the Omaha village and continued onwards up the Missouri. [41]The reader might imagine the growing unease as they paddled further and further from civilization and deeper into Indian Country.

Though both the land and sea expeditions chartered by John Astor suffered multiple fatalities in reaching the Columbia River, the overland journey pushed through astonishing hardships in order to reach their destination. It is not only admirable that the people in this expedition were able to overcome so many difficulties, but it is even more impressive how crucial Indians were to their survival.[42] As will be highlighted many times in their journey, Indians proved to be gifts from Providence rather than dangers to these early pioneers. When tribes did become hostile to white men, it was often with good reason and as an act of retribution.[43]

After receiving warnings from multiple sources, Hunt made the executive decision to steer clear of the notoriously dangerous Blackfoot tribe of the upper Missouri River. This territory which at the time covered much of modern day Northern Montana and Southern Alberta was in reality much larger as the Blackfoot were hunters of migratory Bison and regularly led war parties outside of their true territory.[44]

40 Irving, *Astoria*, 1:226. The first European journal reference to the Omaha tribe was made by Pierre-Charles Le Sueur in 1700. Informed by reports, he described an Omaha village with 400 dwellings and a population of about 4,000 people. It was located on the Big Sioux River near its confluence with the Missouri, near present-day Sioux City, Iowa.

41 Irving, *Astoria*, 1:244.

42 Irving, *Astoria*, 1:129, 135, 143, & 182.

43 John Colter, a member of the Lewis and Clark expedition, said that Meriwether Lewis was at least partially responsible for the Blackfoot's hatred of whites. While exploring Blackfoot territory, they met with several Blackfoots and explained to them that they were in America now and things would be changing. They woke up the next day to find several young Blackfeet trying to steal their rifles and horses (which was a respected practice among adolescents). One of the teens was stabbed and another shot to death. Lewis, in an act assumed to be a warning or declaration of power, left a Jefferson Peace Medal around the neck of one of the dead to be sure there would be no doubt of who killed them. Irving, *Astoria*, 1:105.

44 They were a powerful tribe thanks to their territorial control of the largest protein source in North America: the bison. An estimated sixty million of these great

Robert McGee, scalped by Sioux Chief Little Turtle in 1864.
Photograph by E.E. Henry. Library of Congress.

May 26, 1811

While camped on the banks of the river somewhere along the Southeast borders of modern day Kentucky and South Dakota, Hunt's party spotted a pair of canoes paddling downstream.[45] A gun was fired to grab their attention and request their visit. The men proved to be three veteran hunters of Kentucky. Their names were Edward Robinson, John Hoback and Jacob Rezner and they had been working for the Missouri Fur Company in the upper regions of the Missouri River and Rocky Mountains. What better people for Hunt's party to run into?

It turns out that fate would benefit everyone on this particular day as these three men changed their minds when they saw the well-equipped and staffed company. Right then and there, the three men joined Hunt's party and brought with them crucial information about the Blackfoot tribe

beasts once roamed the plains of Montana and the Dakotas prior to European and American contact. Bureau of Sport Fisheries and Wildlife, "The American Buffalo." *Conservation Note* 12 (January 1965).

45 Irving, *Astoria*, 1:253.

Alfred Jacob Miller (1810–1874). *Indians Threatening to Attack Fur Boats.*
Watercolor on paper, c. 1858. Walters Art Museum.

which lay just upriver from where they now were. One of the trappers, Mr. Robinson, had come to know the tribe on a more personal level than the other two. Robinson had been scalped and left for dead during a skirmish with the Blackfoot Indians and showed everyone the scars to prove it.[46]

As any man who valued his life would, Hunt altered his plans which had been to travel right through the heart of Blackfoot country. Instead, Hunt decided to leave the Missouri River entirely and travel overland in hopes of finding a passage to the Columbia River. To do this, his party would require a new means of transportation as their sturdy keel boats would have to be abandoned with the river. Fortunately, Hunt was informed about the friendly Arikara tribe just upriver that would be willing to trade for their horses.[47]

---

46 Irving, *Astoria*, 1:254.

47 The Arikara tribe originally settled along the Nebraska South Dakota border but eventually migrated to North Dakota seeking mutual protection with the Mandan and Hidatsa tribes from the hostile Sioux and European settlers. They are now federally recognized as the Three Affiliated Tribes of the Fort Berthold Reservation. *http://en.wikipedia.org/wiki/Arikara.*

28

As they rounded a bend they were met by a large party of Sioux warriors that blocked their advancement upriver.[48] After a brief standoff between the horse-mounted Sioux warriors and Hunt's keel boats mounted with howitzers, the Sioux warriors gestured for a parlay to which Hunt accepted.[49] The Sioux chief explained that he would not allow them farther upriver, in an effort to prevent them from trading with the Arikara tribe. With this trade sanction in effect, Hunt's party had little to worry about as they explained through their translator, Pierre Dorion, that they would travel far beyond the Arikara tribe. Satisfied with this knowledge and the gifts provided by Hunt, the Sioux warriors allowed their advancement upriver.[50]

June & July, 1811

It was not long after their peaceful goodbyes with the Sioux warriors that Hunt's party crossed paths with yet another even larger group of Indians mounted on horseback, estimated to be at least 300 in size.[51] Initially, this was quite threatening. After what must have felt like an eternity, a tense standoff ended with the tribe gesturing they wanted to trade by throwing their weapons and buffalo hides down and entering the river to greet Hunt's men.

This particular group of Indians were not hostile to Hunt's party, in fact they were members of the very tribe with whom they were looking to trade.[52] With this understanding, the warriors returned to their village, where they would meet Hunt's party when they arrived in their boats several days later.

The Pacific Fur Company was now over five hundred miles upriver from St. Louis and making great progress towards the Rockies. Imagine their surprise when they were overtaken by another American keelboat, this one led by another large fur company operating out of St. Louis: the Missouri Fur Company.

The scenery was becoming more wild with every day's progress as

---

48 Irving, *Astoria*, 1:264.

49 A howitzer is a short-barreled cannon which, during this time period, was loaded likely with cannon balls and gun powder.

50 Irving, *Astoria*, 1:267.

51 Irving, *Astoria*, 1:277.

52 Even though they had just told the Sioux warriors (who were at war with the Arikara) that they would not trade with them. Irving, *Astoria*, 1:265.

Punka Indians Encamped on the Banks of the Missouri, plate 11 from volume 1 of *Travels in the Interior of North America* by Karl Bodmer. Watercolor on paper, 1843. Joslyn Art Museum, Omaha, Nebraska.

they were now in a land that had been largely untouched.[53] Countless bison grazed within sight of the boats, along with deer, antelope and elk. Finally they reached the settlement of the Arikara tribe and were invited into the chief's lodge to discuss trading. As is the custom in some Native American tribes, they sat down and smoked tobacco from a long pipe. It was arranged that Hunt's party would trade some of its goods[54] for Arikara horses.[55]

53 Irving, *Astoria*, 1:280.

54 Guns, knives, gunpowder, tomahawks, metal pots/pans most desired by Native tribes.

55 Common among many Native American tribes was the status of wealth that horses brought. It was deemed an honorable practice to steal horses from neighboring tribes, capture horses from the wild and even take horses branded by Spaniards. See Irving, *Astoria*, 1:293.

Albert Bierstadt, View of Chimney Rock, Oglillalh Sioux Village in Foreground.
1860. Oil on canvas, Colby College Museum of Art

Unfortunately, the Arikara didn't have enough horses to meet Hunt's needs and so a trade was made between Hunt's party and Lisa's: as Hunt would no longer need his boats, he traded them for horses which were in possession of the Missouri Fur Company at a post upriver. And so the two competing fur trading companies became trading partners at least in this instance, though each helped the other greatly in the transaction.[56]

By mid-July, Hunt was ready to begin his true "overland journey" to the Columbia. Having obtained eighty-two horses and plenty of rest, he decided the safest bet would be to break off from the Lewis and Clark trail to blaze his own.[57] This was a crucial turning point in their journey for it was a departure from the relatively familiar terrain of the Missouri River into the complete unknown. What was waiting for them beyond the distant Rocky Mountains was a landscape so harsh it would claim the lives of several men and nearly bring ruin to the entire expedition.

56 Irving, *Astoria*, 1:304.
57 Which would follow the remainder of the Missouri River through hostile Blackfoot territory and thus jepordize his mission.

Entering Virgin Territory

Hunt's party departed the Missouri River near modern day Mobridge, South Dakota,[58] and began traveling West across the great plains on horseback. It didn't take long before they came upon yet another settlement of tipis on an open prairie. There were horses grazing near by and after some careful consideration, the tribe was determined to be that of the friendly Cheyenne people.[59] After a warm and most hospitable welcome, Hunt exchanged American goods for thirty-six additional horses.[60]

August, 1811

Ten months had passed since Hunt's party originally pushed off from the port of St. Louis. In addition to the sixty people in his party, there was now a train of 118 horses riding across the plains of what is now South Dakota. They were approaching the territory of the Crow tribe, another relatively unknown tribe that in anticipation of trading with, Hunt had hired Edward Rose to be their interpreter.[61] Prior to reaching the Crow peoples, they passed through the challenging landscape of the Black Hills.

The Black Hills were the first real elevation gain since leaving the Missouri River and navigating through them was no easy task. The forests were thick and prime haven to wild game they had never seen before such as black tail deer and big horn sheep.[62] Hunt had a very difficult time finding a suitable passage through the steep hills and eventually decided to climb a tall peak in order to get a better idea of what he was dealing with. In the distant West he could see what he believed to be the Bighorn

---

58 Irving, *Astoria*, 1:304. They left the river from the Arikara tribe settlement which was about 150 miles south of the Mandan villages near modern day Bismark, North Dakota.

59 Cheyenne according to tribal history once settled in the Great Lakes region of Minnesota but were driven Westward by other tribes. Eventually they adopted a nomadic life on the plains and hunted buffalo with the aid of their domesticated horses.

60 Irving, *Astoria*, 1:324.

61 Another language interpreter with a colorful background, he had been a pirate on the Mississippi River, who fled to the wilderness and settled with the Crow and married a woman of the tribe. Astoria by Irving p. 333. Rose was plotting to steal the horses of Hunt's party and desert them before reaching the Crow settlement where he would be able to settle as a rich man with his new stock of horses. Hunt became wary of Rose and as a result, gave him a generous offer of pay and goods that ensured his honesty. See Irving, *Astoria*, 1:340.

62 Irving, *Astoria*, 1:346.

Karl Bodmer. Crow Indians, plate 13 from Vol 1 of *Travels in the Interior of North America*. Watercolor on paper, Private Collection

Mountains so he knew he was on the right course. Being that there was plentiful game about, that also meant there would be a healthy population of large predators.

As they made their way farther into the forest, they saw signs of a healthy grizzly population. One of the experienced hunters of the group, William Cannon, was nearly eaten by one while out looking for game.[63]

Fortunately, Hunt found safe passage through the Black Hills after stumbling upon a well-worn path of the Crow Tribe.[64] This trail took the group over one hundred miles across the hot, dry plains of what would become North Eastern Wyoming. Finally, they reached the Bighorn Mountains where water and game were again plentiful.

On their first evening encamped at the foot of the Bighorn Mountains, a pair of Crow Indians approached them on horseback. Their own Crow interpreter, Edward Rose, was sent out immediately to speak with them on peaceful terms. The two men were determined to be scouts from a Crow village located further into the mountains. After some discussion,

63 Irving, *Astoria*, 1:352.
64 Irving, *Astoria*, 1:356.

34

Hunt's party was escorted to the village and greeted warmly by the chief.[65] Here again they traded highly valued American goods for horses and dried foods. After a night's rest and favorable trading, Hunt departed the Crow village and continued onwards through the mountains.

After struggling for a few days to find a pass, they were joined by a few Crow Indians that had been dispatched from the very village he had just left. It turns out the Chief had sent them to escort Hunt's party through a known pass. This gesture was a certainly a blessing, as the Bighorn Mountains were a difficult range with over a dozen twelve thousand foot peaks.[66]

September, 1811

With the Bighorn mountains behind them, Hunt's party reached the Bighorn river which the guides in his party assured would lead them south to the mouth of the Wind River and from there on a westerly course to the

65 Irving, *Astoria*, 1:364.
66 Irving, *Astoria*, 1:369.

headwaters of the Columbia River.[67] But before they would see anything on the Pacific slope, they would have to pass through the mighty Teton mountain range in northwestern Wyoming.[68]

This is the land of liberty and equality, where a man sees and feels that he is a man merely, and that he can no longer exist, except if he can himself procure the means of support.

Robert Stuart, journal postscript
for October 13, 1812, while
starving in Wyoming

They were entering a country more wild and untamed than they had ever seen before. It was so remote that they didn't see any signs of human life for days on end. When they finally did spot a couple of Indians, the pair quickly fled into the forest when they saw Hunt's large party. Mr. Hunt chased after them and eventually learned why they were so afraid: apparently they had never seen a white man before.[69] After communicating through simple gestures, it was determined they were part of the Snake or Shoshone tribe and were settled with a larger group nearby.

Fortunately Hunt was invited to visit the settlement where he would be able to add to his rations. In addition to delicious buffalo jerky, Hunt also traded for the first beaver pelts of the trip which he paid generously for. This would help plant a seed with the Shoshone that beavers were extremely valuable and that Hunt's group would be back again to buy more. Additionally, Hunt hired two Shoshones to guide his party to a nearby post called Fort Henry which had been recently abandoned.

Brother Andrew Henry (1775-1832)

In 1809, brother Andrew Henry joined with Manuel Lisa, brother Jean Pierre Chouteau and brother William Clark to found the Missouri Fur Company. In an effort to establish his company and the first trading posts on the upper Missouri River, Henry led an expedition up the Missouri river in the summer of 1809. From the Missouri he branched off onto the Yellowstone River and then wintered at the mouth of the Bighorn river

67 Irving, *Astoria*, 1:380.

68 Five of the principal mountains of this range, sometimes referred to as the "Cathedral group," are over 12,000 feet tall.

69 Irving, *Astoria*, 1:385.

about (fifty miles east of modern day Billings, Montana). Along the way, he and his party established several posts at strategic locations for fur trading but the most important being at the three forks of the Missouri.

When the river thawed the next spring, Henry returned to the Three Forks post where he was brutally attacked by Blackfoot Indians causing his group to split up. Some fled immediately back downriver to St. Louis while others stayed under the command of Henry and defended the post. After a few days of holding off the Blackfeet, Henry and his men were

outnumbered by over two hundred warriors causing them to flee to the south and out of Blackfoot territory.[70]

All was not lost, they were still in an area rich with beavers. Even though they had just been nearly killed by the Blackfoot, there were huge fortunes at stake. They ended up following the Madison River to the North Fork of the Snake River where they built a fort in hopes of settling

70 *http://en.wikipedia.org/wiki/Missouri_Fur_Company.*

in.[71] This section of river would from thence be called "Henrys Fork" and the fort they built called "Fort Henry." Fort Henry was at this time the furthest American fur trading post west of St. Louis. After all the work they would put into building it, the fort would have to be abandoned in the spring of 1811 due to a lack of food available in the area. Interestingly, it only sat neglected for a few months before Hunt's party arrived and made use of it.

October, 1811

While it would have surely been preferred that they come across a fully functioning trading post with food, whiskey and furs this far into their journey instead what the abandoned post meant was that Mr. Astor's Pacific Fur Company was now in the lead for claiming the Columbia River. The simple wooden huts found at Fort Henry were now occupied by Astor's Pacific Fur Company which was a huge accomplishment but they still had a long way to go. So far in fact, that they still had another 800 miles of terrain to cover before they would reach the mouth of the Columbia.

It was here on the North Fork of the Snake River that Hunt would be able to put the French voyageurs to work paddling down the Snake River. Hunt was hopeful he could take this river directly to the Columbia but soon realized that rivers were of a different temperament this side of the Rockies.

After ten days of camping at Fort Henry, Hunt's men constructed fifteen canoes from the plentiful trees to be found near the site.[72] They opted to leave their horses behind with the two Shoshone guides and pushed their heavily loaded canoes off and into the unknown river. Evidence of the region's inhospitable nature soon became obvious as they went for nearly week without seeing any Indian settlements.

Finally, on the 24th of October, they rejoiced upon seeing a camp of Shoshones. The Shoshones had different feelings about seeing fifteen canoes full of starving white men coming down their river. Either it was the first time they had ever seen white men or they were just exercising a

---

71 The post was located on what is now called Henrys Fork, a tributary river of the Snake River in southeastern Idaho. It is also referred to as the North Fork of the Snake River.

72 Irving, *Astoria*, 2:8.

Alfred Jacob Miller. *Wild scenery (Making a cache).*
Watercolor on paper, 1858. The Walters Art Gallery, Baltimore.

natural caution but they bolted off into the forest.[73]

The remote region they were now passing through (Southeastern Idaho) was inhabited by very primitive nomadic peoples of the Shoshone tribe. At this settlement, the clerks in Hunt's party noted great quantities of small fish two inches long in their tents along with roots, seeds and grain which they were drying for winter. They appeared to be destitute of working tools but had impressive bows and arrows that were well made. There were also carrying vessels of willow and grass to transport water. Imagine how valuable a few knives were to this tribe when they were left by Hunt's party.[74] Further, consider the effect this simple gesture would have on the Shoshone people about the strange white men passing down their river.

After leaving the Shoshone encampment, Hunt's group of canoes paddled down river in a manner that was far more preferable than riding through the rocky terrain on horseback. All was going according to plan until the 28th of October, when they experienced the first tragedy of the

73 Irving, *Astoria*, 2:18.
74 Ibid.

expedition.

The river which had been calm and wide now narrowed and was full of huge boulders. With each bend, it became more dangerous and further tested the skills of the voyageurs. Eventually they met their match when they came to a particular set of rapids. One of the heavy canoes was unable to get around a boulder and its hull was split in half. All five men aboard were launched into the water along with their precious cargo. Of the men, four were able to swim to safety but one perished in the rapids.[75] This loss brought everyone to a halt. The voyageurs needed time to regroup and Hunt had to determine if it was safe to continue downriver.[76]

At this point they had paddled over two hundred miles down the Snake River and were now officially lost in a landscape largely devoid of life. Indeed, they were the first recorded non-indigenous people to ever see this part of the world.

With the river frothing and churning below them, the surrounding land looked nearly as formidable. It was barren and harsh, all rocks and sage brush for as far as the eyes could see. Bro. Hunt ordered a camp to be set up here at the rapids (nicknamed by the French voyageurs the "Cauldron Linn") and dispatched small groups to scout the area. They needed

75 Irving, *Astoria*, 2:20.

76 From St. Anthony to Cauldron Linn (modern day Murtaugh, Idaho) was roughly 200 miles.

to determine if there was any hope of the river returning to a peaceful course, if their were any nearby tribes to trade with or if there might be an alternative route to take.

The reports that came back were grim: the river continued cascading through the canyons for miles, there were no Indians to be found nearby and there were no trails to follow. Faced with a difficult decision, Hunt split the group in half. They now set out in opposite directions, hoping to find a way to the Columbia River.

The Group Splits up and Battles Starvation

Hunt was now in charge of a smaller party of some 31 men, one (now very pregnant) Native American woman and her two small children aged two and four.[77] Aside from their fourteen canoes, there was still a large amount of gear with them including their trading goods such as kettles, pots, knives, guns and gun powder as well as their trapping provisions. At this point in their journey, Hunt decided to cache much of their gear as they now would be carrying everything on foot.

The remaining food rations consisted of forty pounds of Indian corn, twenty pounds of grease and about one hundred and fifty pounds of dried meat for the whole crew of thirty.[78] No one in the group had any idea where they were. In modern reality, they were along the southern border of Idaho, and still hundreds of miles from the Columbia River.

The two parties set out praying they would find food and shelter. After a few days of fruitless searching they came upon an Indian trail which they followed to a nearby village. Hunt's men happily traded knives for dried salmon which was a welcome change from their usual dried meats. It is likely that this was the first time many in Hunt's group had ever tasted salmon in their lives. As it was now November, the fall salmon run was in full force and the nutritious fish would become a regular part of their diet.

They continued on foot downriver and even though they often ran into a Shoshone here and there, none could answer whether they were heading in the right direction. December arrived and brought with it bone chilling winds and snow. Hunt now resorted killing their pack horses for

77 Irving, *Astoria*, 2:43.
78 Irving, *Astoria*, 2:35.

food as their rations were nearly out.[79]

On December the 6th, Hunt's group made out the silloutes of a group on the opposite side of the river. It was Mr. Crooks who was in charge of a small search party that had split off from Hunt's at the Cauldron Linn rapids. They shouted across the river pleading for food. Hunt sent what little horse meat he could spare across with a voyageur in a small canoe.[80]

After filling on some horse meat, Mr. Crooks explained what had transpired since he split up from Hunt some twenty days before. He and his group had been fruitlessly searching for a path, living off of half rations, the meat of one beaver and even the leather soles on their moccasins![81] Finally when they had nearly lost all hope of survival they saw Hunt and his party and yelled for help.

Brother Hunt now had to decide what to do with his now larger group of starving men, woman and children. He could continue onwards hoping to stumble upon another Indian encampment or turn back and look for the nearest encampment they had passed. He opted for the latter and with his crew of now desperately starving souls he turned back in his course in search of a Shoshone camp.

Fortunately they came upon an encampment sooner than expected. Even better was the fact that they had horses which were now solely desired for their meat. They approached the encampment by surprise and seized five of the horses. One was said to be killed immediately and cooked over a fire while the other four were spared for another day. For the Indians who had just been robbed of five prized horses, Hunt left several items which he said were worth far more than the animals.

Hunt now reassessed the situation and knew he couldn't delay their progress any longer. He decided to continue downriver now with his original party and two horses. He left the other two horses with Mr. Crooks and his famished men who were too weak to continue on downriver with Hunt. Within a few days Hunt came to another Shoshone camp, this one made up of twelve huts on the banks of a tributary stream.

Here Hunt was grateful to learn that had his party continued down the Snake River they would surely starve to death. Instead, the good people informed him of another way up over the mountains and to the "Great

79 Irving, *Astoria*, 2:49.

80 Horse skin canoe: crafted in Indian fashion and made from the skin of the horse they had eaten the night before. See Irving, *Astoria*, 2:51.

81 Irving, *Astoria*, 2:52.

River."[82]

Hunt thanked them for the advice but really needed someone to show him the way. It was now late November and these Shoshone peoples were just slowing down for the winter when they would subsist on dried fish, roots and grains. For this reason, it was not easy for Hunt to hire someone willing to guide his party over the snowy mountains.

He ended up offering two guns, three knives, and two horses to anyone "man enough" to take him over the mountains.[83] This offer was too good to pass up and so again the group was saved by helpful Indians.

Departure from the Snake River

December, 1811

They were blazing a course through the Blue Mountains on what would only decades later become the Oregon Trail (now Interstate 84 in Oregon). It was the dead of winter, snow was waist-deep at times and Hunt's group of thirty souls were now being pushed to their limits. To make things even more troubling, Marie Dorion, the only woman in the group, gave birth—without, of course, any medicine or professional help— to a child that she would need to care for in addition to her other two children. It is hard to imagine anyone in the group was optimistic at the addition of a newborn.[84]

Despite their provisions running low, hope was restored upon the sight of yet another Shoshone encampment. At this camp, Hunt traded guns and ammunition for horses which were immediately slaughtered for food. It was now New Years Eve of 1811, a favorite holiday of the French Voyageurs and so Hunt granted them an additional day off to celebrate. A roaring fire was made, fresh meat was roasted and traditional voyageur songs were sung, surely lifting the spirits of the group.

---

82 Although they were still relatively far from the Columbia River, most Indians in the Pacific Northwest knew of the Columbia River or its general whereabouts. This type of information was invaluable to Hunt and his men.

83 Irving, *Astoria*, 2:66.

84 Unfortunately this child did not survive. Within a few weeks it passed away. See Irving, *Astoria*, 2:77.

It is estimated they were now near the modern day town of La Grande, Oregon.[85] The Shoshones informed them that the Cayuse Indians were just a few days march beyond the Blue Mountains.[86]

It's All Downhill From Here

January 1812

The Blue Mountains were not nearly as tall as the Rockies, but the group still had to battle deep snow and fierce cold. After many difficult days of trudging, they came to a lookout in the forest.[87] One can only imagine their excitement when they looked out across a sloping valley to see more horses and tipis than they could possibly count. As Hunt and his men grew closer to the tribe, they noticed brass and copper kettles warming over fires, steel axes, and other items that could only come from one place: the Pacific Ocean trade.

Indeed they were close, two days in fact from the great river according to the Cayuse Indians with whom they were staying. Several days were spent recovering amongst the friendly tribe. Surely these weary travelers were grateful to feast on fresh meat, to smoke tobacco, and to warm themselves by a fire. A few members of Hunt's group were said to have eaten so much they actually got sick.[88] Either way, they were happy to be alive and out of the cold.

Brother Hunt always concerned about the well being of his men, became even more elated upon hearing from the Cayuse that another small party of white men had just been through their camp. It was surely the rest of the original party which had split off from Hunt at the Cauldrin Linn! M'Kenzie, M'Lellan and their party were alive and just a few days ahead of Hunt.

After several days of rest, they followed the Umatilla River which

---

85 The Grande Ronde Valley in which La Grande, Oregon, sits was later used as a waypoint along the Oregon Trail.

86 A range in the Columbia River Plateau located in eastern Oregon. This would be the final mountain range to test emigrants later on the Oregon Trail. Highest peaks include Rock Peak Butte (9,106 feet), Strawberry Mountain (9,038 feet) and Mount Ireland (8,304 feet). *https://en.wikipedia.org/wiki/Blue_Mountains_(Pacific_Northwest)*.

87 Cayuse Indians were at this time a nomadic hunting tribe that lived in teepees. They were well clothed in buffalo and deer hides as they were very successful hunters and skilled horsemen.

88 Irving, *Astoria*, 2:77.

Alfred Jacob Miller - Encampment of Shoshone Indians, Green River, WY. 1837.
Watercolor on paper, Gilcrease Museum, OK

they were told fed into the Columbia. Finally, on the 21st of January, 1812, sixteen months after they first departed St. Louis, they took in the magnificent blue waters of the Columbia River.

What a relief it must have been to finally see the river after everything they had gone through. All they had to do now was follow its course to Fort Astoria where the real work would begin.

The Columbia River Indians

Camped along side this great river were many Indian tribes of various living conditions. All were unique to this particular region and are classified by anthropologists as the Plateau Indians. The main tribes of the plateau region were the Nez Perce, Yakima, Spokane, Cayuse and Wishram peoples. When brothers Lewis and Clark passed through this area in 1805, they were the first to establish friendly relations with nearly all of them.[89]

If the Shoshone people were primitive because of their isolated location, these Plateau Indians were advanced and well versed in trading with each other. It is estimated that the overall indigenous population for the entire region was well over 180,000 people at the time Hunt was passing

89 Harry Ritter, *Washington's History: The People, Land, and Events of the Far Northwest* (Portland: WestWinds Press, 2003), 20.

through.[90] This is not surprising when we consider that the Columbia River provided a seemingly unlimited supply of salmon each year like clockwork. Tragically, as European diseases made their way up the Columbia River by way of the fur trade, the original large Indian population was quickly decimated. Only a tiny percentage of the original population was still alive by the time the first covered wagons started to arrive.

About 100 miles down the banks of the Columbia they reached to the Dalles.[91] This unique location was essentially the great Indian trading emporium of the entire region. At this site every spring and summer, thousands of Indians would congregate from all over the Pacific Northwest to trade, fish, gamble, and socialize with one another.[92]

Because there were so many different people assembled here from all over the Columbia River region, it is not surprising that Hunt was able to get some very interesting news about the destination he was headed for. Rumors had already been circulating at the Dalles that a group of white traders built a "great house" at the mouth of the Columbia and were waiting for the rest of their group to join them from upriver.

February, 1812

The arrival of Hunt's party at the Dalles must have caused quite a stir among the locals. After several days of parlay, Hunt was able to trade his horses for dugout canoes which would surely carry them the rest of the way down river. Thanks to the strong current of the Columbia and the steady paddling of the voyageurs, they finally reached the mouth of the Columbia ten days later. Imagine the mixture of exhaustion and joy they must have felt when they first saw the fledgling American settlement they had just traveled so far to reach.

The Mouth of the Columbia

After crossing the barren plains, the jagged Rocky Mountains and the Martian landscape of the Snake River, Hunt's group had reached Fort Astoria to join the rest of the Pacific Fur Company. No longer would they be forced to pack up each morning and continue trudging towards a distant

---

90 Oscar Winther, *The Old Oregon Country: A History of Frontier Trade, Transportation and Travel* (Stanford, Calif.: Stanford University Press, 1950), 8.

91 French for "Flat Stones" or "Flat Stone Rapids" and currently a city in Oregon State.

92 Ritter, Washington's History, 21.

Paul Kane (1810–1871). *Flat-Head Woman and Child.*
Oil on Canvas, 1848. Montreal Museum of Fine Arts.

horizon. They had survived and now the real work was about to begin.

Fortunately for everyone in Hunt's group, construction of the fort had already begun thanks to the other crew which had arrived earlier by ship. In addition to the foundations for the fort, they had already established a relationship with the Chinook tribe who lived just across the river from Fort Astoria. This meant business had already begun by the time Hunt arrived.

John Stanley. Mount Hood from the Dalles.
Oil on canvas, 1871. Courtesy of the University of Michigan Museum of Art

The Chinook Tribe

The Chinook tribe was made up of less than 500 people at this time and was led by a chief named Comcomly.[93] Comcomly and the Chinook tribe overall were already well experienced in trading with white men prior to even Lewis and Clark's arrival to the area.

When the Pacific Fur Company's ship arrived in 1810, one of the clerks took extensive notes on the Chinook people he met with. The notes below are taken directly from one such journal:

> [The Chinook are] of low stature, few of them passing five feet six inches, and many of them not even five feet. They pluck out the beard…we were surprised to see that they had almost all flattened heads. This configuration is not a natural deformity, but an effect of art, caused by compression of the skull in infancy. It shocks strangers extremely, especially at first sight; nevertheless…it is an indispensable ornament…it was only slaves who had not their heads flattened. The natives of the Columbia procure these slaves from the neighboring tribes and from the interior, in exchange for beads and furs. They treat them with humanity

93 Robert Stuart & Kenneth A. Spaulding, *On the Oregon Trail: Robert Stuart's Journey of Discovery* (Ann Arbor, Mi.: UMI, 1991), 28.

Mysteries Among the Indigenous Americans

Among the Coast Salish peoples were fully developed secret societies, formal complex clan development and initiations involving scarification.The Chinooks appear to have had no such societies by the time of contact with whites.[1]

This apparently was found with east coast tribes as well such as the Iroquois. In his *Encyclopædia of Freemasonry,* Albert Mackey wrote of the "American Mysteries," recording that a society had been found claiming to be in existence since creation which was composed of a select number of initiates.[2]

In the twentieth century, Bro. Arthur C. Parker (1881–1955), an archaeologist and museum director who was also a Seneca Indian has also argued for the relevance of ceremonial parallels between Freemasonry and Native traditions.[3]

1   Verne F. Ray, "The Historical Position of the Lower Chinook in the Native Culture of the Northwest." Pacific Northwest Quarterly 28 (1937): 371.

2   Albert G. Mackey, *An Encyclopædia of Freemasonry and its Kindred Sciences* (Philadelphia: Moss & Co., 1879), 62.

3   Arthur C. Parker, *American Indian Freemasonry* (Albany, N.Y.: Buffalo Consistory, 1919). For academic research about Arthur C. Parker and the perceived interplay between Native American and Masonic traditions, see Chip Colwell-Chanthaphonh, *Inheriting The Past: The Making Of Arthur C. Parker and Andigenous Archaeology* (Tucson: University of Arizona Press, 2009); Joy Porter, *To be Indian: The Life of Iroquois-Seneca Arthur Caswell Parker* (Norman, Ok. : Univ. of Oklahoma Press, 2001); and Joy Porter, *Native American Freemasonry: Associationalism and Performance in America* (Lincoln, Neb.: University of Nebraska Press, 2011).

while their services are useful, but as soon as they become incapable of labor, neglect them and suffer them to perish of want.

The Indians of the Columbia are…above all excellent swimmers…and unlike other American Indians, the Flatheads regard intoxicating drinks as poisons and drunkenness as disgraceful.

The men go entirely naked, not concealing any part of their bodies.

Mark Myers. *The Garden of Eden.*
2001. Courtesy of Mark Myers.

Only in the winter do they throw over their shoulders a skin. The men are not lazy, especially during the fishing season.

Their canoes are all made of cedar, and of a single trunk: we saw some which were five feet wide at the midships, and thirty feet in length; these are the largest, and will carry from twenty-five to thirty men; the smallest will carry but two or three.

Their houses, constructed of cedar, are remarkable for their form and size: some of them are one hundred feet in length by thirty or forty feet in width.

It will be asked, no doubt, what instruments they use in the construction of their canoes and houses…we did not find among them a single hatchet: their only tools consisted of an inch or half-inch chisel and a mallet, which was nothing but an oblong stone. With these wretched implements, they would undertake to cut down the largest cedars of the forest. Such achievements with such means, are a marvel of ingenuity and patience.

The politics of the natives of the Columbia are a simple affair: each village has its chief, but that chief does not seem to exercise a great authority over his fellow-citizens. The chiefs are considered in proportion to their riches: such a chief has a great many wives, slaves and strings of beads—he is accounted a great chief.

…differences sometimes arise, whether between chiefs or the tribes…on these occasions (they) enter into parley, and do all they can to

Paul Kane (1810–1871). *Chinook Indians in Front of Mount Hood.*
Oil on canvas, 1851. National Gallery of Canada, Ottawa, Ontario.

terminate the affair amicably: sometimes a third party becomes mediator between the first two. If those who seek justice do not obtain it to their satisfaction, they retire to some distance, and the combat begins…but as one or two men are killed, the party which has lost these, owns itself beaten and the battle ceases.

Polygamy is permitted, indeed is customary; there are some who have as many as four or five wives.[94]

The Chinook tribe are to be regarded as the original traders, trappers and travelers of the Columbia River. Each tribe in the region had its own economy but the Chinook tribe developed a true currency in the form of long white sea shells called higua.[95] These shells were strung together and commanded high trade value, one transaction observed by an Astorian

94 Gabriel Franchère, *Narrative of a Voyage to the Northwest Coast of America in the years 1811, 1812, 1813* (New York: Redfield, 1854), 324–33.

95 Also called ioquas. These shells were found only in Cape Flattery and there at the bottom of the sea. Indians in canoes would dip long long poles into the sea where they were plunged into the seafloor where the shells lived. The shells were put on a string which determined their value. Forty shells generally measured six feet which was equal in value to a beaver skin. If thirty nine shells measured six feet then it was equal to two beaver skins, and if thirty eight, three skins. See Paul Kane, *Wanderings of an Artist Among the Indians of North America* (London: Longman, Brown, Green, Longmans & Roberts, 1859), 239.

Four unidentified young Indian men with large salmon.
Sir Henry Wellcome Collection, 1856–1936.
National Archives and Records Administration.

clerk saw a brand new gun turned down in exchange for six of these simple shells.[96]

Besides animal furs and higua shells, the Chinooks had direct access to another resource that was both plentiful and highly valuable. The Chinook (also called King) salmon ran right up the Columbia River in seemingly unlimited numbers and are considered by some to be the best tasting fish in the world. Prior to commercial fishing, the natural runs of King salmon would have included whole schools of fish over one hundred pounds each.[97]

The Chinook tribe developed whole rituals and taboos concerning the first salmon caught in the season.[98] Because the fish came up the river at predictable times each year, tribes settled along the Columbia had to just be ready with their spears, nets and baskets at those times. But what about when there were no salmon to be caught in the rivers? The Indians developed a food item unique to the region called salmon pemmican which is essentially sun dried salmon beaten to a powder and then compressed together into blocks of up to ten pounds. Through this method, the nutrient-rich fish could be preserved for several years and transported great distances creating a valuable trade item.

Besides salmon, there was a smaller more peculiar fish utilized by Columbia River tribes known as the candlefish (also called eulachon fish). This "candlefish" derives its name from it being so filled with fatty oils that if caught, dried, and strung on a wick, it could be burned as a candle. The candle fish could also be rendered into a heavy grease (similar to bacon grease) which did not spoil and could thus travel great distances.

The grease in turn became a highly valuable trade item for Indians of the region. Over time, vast trade networks were established all over the region. Trails were worn in the forest and aptly called "grease trails" for the fact that they were used to move this precious grease inland to other tribes.[99] These same grease trails would later be used by Americans emigrants as they began to move in and settle in the region. Surely the early pioneers were grateful to follow these well-worn trails in otherwise

96 Winther, *The Old Oregon Country*, 10.

97 Roberta Ulrich, *Empty Nets: Indians, Dams, and the Columbia River* (Corvallis: Oregon State University Press, 1999).

98 Erna Gunther, "An Analysis of the First Salmon Ceremony," *American Anthropologist*, n.s. 28 (October–December, 1926), 605.

99 Winther, *The Old Oregon Country*, 13

impenetrable forest and brush.

In short, trade in the Pacific Northwest began long before the white man came. The Indians who resided in the Pacific Northwest were experienced traders and not easily duped by those who came expecting much in exchange for very little. With that being said, the items that fur traders brought with them to trade were of great use to Indians. Iron pots and pans, copper kettles, wool blankets and other common household items were extremely valuable in a culture that otherwise had no access to these things. Since the Chinooks were strategically located right at the mouth of the river, they also knew they had the first shot at trading with the American and European ships as they arrived. For this reason, they were eager to be the first and only tribe trading with the Pacific Fur Company.

1811
to
1814

Astoria
and Beyond

The First Few Years at Fort Astoria

With their heroic two thousand mile journey now behind them, Hunt's group joined the rest of the Pacific Fur Company at Fort Astoria.[1] By the time Hunt's overland group staggered in during the Spring of 1812, Fort Astoria had already been under construction for nearly a year.[2] Thanks to Bro. Astor's foresight in sending one crew by land and one by sea, the foundation was set on America's first colony in the West.

The Sea Route to Astoria: 1811

Approximately eleven months before Hunt arrived, Astor's ship the *Tonquin* dropped its anchor in the Columbia River near the chosen site for Fort Astoria. The ship had just sailed over twenty thousand miles around the Cape of South America from New York City to reach the Columbia River. On board the ship were an interesting mix of Scottish Fur traders, Canadian Voyageurs, Hawaiian laborers and American sailors.[3] It may seem that this crew got the better deal when compared to Hunt's overland journey but they actually suffered more losses in the end.[4] On the very last part of their trip while crossing the dreaded Columbia River bar, eight crew men from the *Tonquin* drowned.[5]

This particularly ferocious section of the Pacific Ocean is one of nature's

1   The men in charge of Fort Astoria or any other fur trading post were called "partners" or shareholders in the company they worked for. Operating under them were clerks who managed all the accounting, journals and inventory. Under the clerks were the handlers who often were Canadian Voyageurs. This form of hierarchy was how all the major fur companies operated. The three biggest fur companies at this time were the Northwest Company headquartered in Montreal, Hudson Bay Company headquartered in London and the American Fur Company headquartered in New York City. All three were poised to claim the Pacific Northwest region, particularly the Columbia River.

2   Five miles to the southwest lay the ruins of Fort Clatsop, the temporary shelter built during the Lewis and Clark expedition.

3   Their journey required a stop in Honolulu, Hawaii, to restock provisions, hire more crew and of course catch some much needed refreshment. Here they hired twenty-four Hawaiians to work at the fort and purchased one hundred piglets from King Kamehameha. See Stark, *Astoria*, 65).

4   Rations for the partners (this would be worse for the other people) on the ship were daily: a pint and a half of water, 14 oz. hard bread, 1.25 lbs salted beef or pork, a half pint of souchong tea with sugar; weekly: one day of rice and beans, one day of corn meal and molasses; on Sundays a bottle of Teneriffe wine. See Franchère, *Narrative of a Voyage to the Northwest Coast*, 36.

5   Stark, *Astoria*, 88.

Mark Meyers. *We Passed the Boat.*
Watercolor on paper, 2001. Courtesy of Mark Myers.

most volatile creations. The Columbia River Bar is essentially the deadly result of the river smashing head on into the ocean without the buffer of a delta. This impact creates huge rapids as the river blasts like a fire hose into the powerful Pacific Ocean. As the result of all this turbulence, just underneath the surface large sand bars are kicked up from the currents. The combination of violent waves and shifting sand bars makes navigation up the river extremely difficult. Passage is only possible through locating and following the river channel which is what some of the crew from the *Tonquin* were attempting to find when their boat capsized. To this day, only highly skilled "bar pilots" are allowed to guide ships up the channel.[6]

Once the *Tonquin* made it safely across the bar, the crew aboard the had to determine the ideal location for a trading post. This was a very important decision as they had to consider the site's proximity to Indians, the flood plain of the river, adequate views of incoming ships and access to a safe harbor. After much consideration, they decided upon the site which modern day Astoria, Oregon, sits.[7]

6   *https://en.wikipedia.org/wiki/Maritime_pilot.*
7   The original site of this fort is now an interpretive park open to the public.

Facts About the *Tonquin*

300 ton ship. Crew of 21, with 33 passengers.

Partners in the PFC:
Alexander M'Kay, Canada
Duncan M'Dougall, Canada
David Stuart, Canada
Robert Stuart, Canada

Clerks:
James Lewis of NY
Russel Farnham of MA
William W. Matthews of NY
Alexander Ross Canada
Donald M'Gillis Canada
Ovide de Montigny Canada
Francis B. Pillot Canada
Donald M'Lennan Canada
William Wallace Canada
Thomas M'Kay Canada
Gabriel Franchere, Canada

Voyageurs (all from Canada):
Oliver Roy Lapensee
Ignace Lapensee
Basile Lapensee
Jacques Lafantaiseie
Benjamin Roussel
Michel Laframboise
Giles Leclerc
Joseph Lapierre
Joseph Nadeau
J B'te Belleau
Antoine Belleau
Louis Brusle
P.D. Jeremie

Craftsman:
Johann Koaster, ship carpenter from Russia
George Bell, Copper smith, NY
Job Aitken, rigger and calker, Scotland
Augustus Roussil, blacksmith, Canada
Guilleaume Perreault, a boy

Crew:
Jonathan Thorn, captain, NY
Ebenezer D. Fox, 1st mate, Boston
John M. Mumford, 2nd mate, Massachusetts
James Thorn, brother of captain, NY
John Anderson, boatswain, unknown
Egbert Vanderhuff, tailor, NY
John Weeks, carpenter
Stephen Weeks, armorer, NY
John Coles, sailmaker, NY
John Martin, sailmaker, France
John White, Sailor, NY
Adam Fisher, sailor, NY
Peter Verbel, Sailor, NY
Edward Aymes, sailor, NY
Robert Hill, Albany, NY
John Adams, sailor, NY
Joseph Johnson, sailor, Englishman
Charles Roberts, sailor, NY
Unnamed African American cook
Unnamed African American steward

Louis Choris. *Port of Honolulu.*
Lithograph, 1816. Published in *Voyage Pittoresque du Autour du Monde*, Paris.

During the first few months at the site, a patch of land was cleared and the first timber walls were set in place. The landscape they were in didn't exactly lend them any favors. First and foremost was the task of chopping down mighty cedar trees which had been growing there for centuries.[8] However, if their Indian neighbors across the river could bring them down with primitive tools, surely the Astorians could with steel-headed axes.[9]

Aside from building a secure fort, relationships had to be established with local tribes to get trade going. Mr. McDougal and Mr. Stuart were the first to paddle across the river and introduce themselves to the Chinook tribe. The two seasoned traders were received with great hospitality by the Chief, Comcomly.[10] It was, of course good business on both sides to be cordial in this first encounter.

Even though the Pacific Fur Company was new to the region, Comcomly and the Chinook Indians were well acquainted with American and British traders by this point. It is estimated that in 1792 alone, there were no less than twenty ships that visited the Pacific Northwest Coast in

8 Stuart & Spaulding, *On the Oregon Trail*, 31. Some cedars were as large as fifty feet in circumference.

9 Canoe making had been a long standing tradition among the Indians of the Columbia River. First a suitable cedar tree was selected then slowly chipped away at with stone chisels, similar to how a beaver works its way around a trunk. From James G. Swan, *The Northwest Coast; or Three Years' Residence in Washington Territory* (New York: Harper, 1857), 79-82.

10 Irving, *Astoria*, 1:115.

search of furs.[11] One particular ship during that year, the *Columbia*, led by an American Captain of the name Robert Gray, successfully navigated the Columbia Bar and became the first ship to ever document the Columbia River. Captain Gray is likely to have met Chief Comcomly during his visit when he traded with the Chinooks in May of 1792. Because of contact like this, the Chief and the tribe overall would get a taste of what was to come with big ships coming up their river looking for precious furs.

Evidence of the Chinook people's contact with white maritime traders was even apparent to Lewis and Clark who noted Caucasian features on two Indians they met. They may, one imagines, have experienced some bewilderment when arriving at the edge of the known world and finding an Indian with red hair, freckles, and a tattoo which read "Jack Ramsey."[12] This story has been debated ever since and if true, would suggest that the river had been explored by European ships prior to American ones.

While treacherous, the mouth of the Columbia River was essentially

11   Irving, *Astoria*, 1:30.

12   John C. Jackson, *Children of the Fur Trade: Forgotten Métis of the Pacific Northwest* (Missoula, Mont.: Mountain Press, 1995), 6; *The Journals of Lewis and Clark Expedition*, vol. 6, November 2, 1805–March 22, 1806.

the doorway to riches and Astor's Pacific Fur Company was now in prime position to control it. After setting up a basic defensive post at the fort, a decision was made to dispatch the heavily armed PFC ship the *Tonquin* to other trading sites in the region. It was just two months after it arrived that the *Tonquin* pulled up its anchor and sailed back out into the Pacific and headed north to Vancouver Island. Little did anyone on the ship know that not one person who left that day would ever return.[13]

The Tonquin's final journey: June, 1811

In command of the *Tonquin* was thirty-one-year-old Captain Jonathan Thorn who lacked familiarity of the region and its customs but was a skilled captain. In addition to the *Tonquin's* crew were experienced fur traders that would be able to negotiate with the tribes they would encounter. To further ensure their success, they stopped in Grays Harbor on the way up the coast and hired an interpreter named Josechal who was familiar with the Indians of the region.[14] One of the first things Josechal told his new employers was that the Indians they intended to trade with were not on friendly terms with European or American traders.[15]

It turned out that in the particular area they were headed for on Vancouver Island (Clayoquot Sound) was a band of the Nootka tribe that had been brutally attacked by Captain Robert Gray in 1792. As a result of this attack, the tribe was ready for retribution. Unfortunately for all of the crew aboard the ship, this was of little concern to Captain Thorn who believed the *Tonquin* had enough firepower to defend against any Indian attack. Besides, Captain Thorn had direct instructions to stock the ship with furs to take to Canton, China. This stop would be just one of many to fill the ship with furs destined for the Asian market.

13   Irving, *Astoria*, 1:123.
14   Stark, *Astoria*, 201.
15   Stark, *Astoria*, 202.

The Pacific side of Vancouver Island once supported a large Indian population given the rich biodiversity of the environment. One of the more powerful tribes on the Island were the Nootka who became big players in the maritime fur trade. Their first contact with European ships occurred as early as Captain Cook's visit in 1778. Since that contact, fur trade had grown increasingly important to their livelihood. The man who most realized that importance was Chief Wickanannish, a powerful leader that became wealthy by trading with European and American ships.[16]

Even if Captain Thorn had been more experienced in trading he still wouldn't have been prepared for the Nootka peoples. The Nootka were near the top of the list for the most powerful tribes in the entire Pacific Northwest. Similar to how the Blackfoot Indians of Montana were in territorial control of millions of bison, the Nootka Indians of West Vancouver Island lived in one of the richest and most biologically diverse areas on the planet. All around Vancouver Island were seemingly unlimited supplies of whales, salmon, shellfish, herring, cod, halibut, sardines, seals, sea lions, porpoise as well as deer, bears and elk.

Additionally, the Nootka Indians became master craftsman in woodworking. They carved ornate canoes, totem poles and massive long houses out of the rich forest that surrounded them.[17]

In 1788, during one of the first documented visits to Clayquot Sound by a British Captain by the name of John Meares, a detailed description of the inhabitants of the region and their leader, Chief Wikanannish was made. The powerful chief was described as a man in his early forties, of athletic build and in control of a region of well over 10,000 Indians with its principle village, Opitsat, settled by over 4,000 people.[18]

Just four years later in 1792, this prospering village was completely destroyed by Captain Robert Gray while on the same expedition in which he explored the Columbia River. He rationalized this act as a defensive move because he believed Chief Wikanannish wanted to commandeer his ship in order to go to war with neighboring tribes. Whatever caused him to retaliate is up to speculation, but it sure that Captain Gray ordered

---

16 Margaret Horsfield & Ian Kennedy, *Tofino and Clayoquot Sound: A History* (Madeira Park, B.C.: Harbour Publishing, 2014), 64.

17 Stark, *Astoria*, 204.

18 The site of this village was on modern day Meares Island, one of the many islands surrounding the village of Tofino, British Columbia.

the destruction of this original settlement. With this event in mind, we can understand why Josechal warned Captain Thorn about attempting to trade with the tribe.

Everything started out just fine as lead fur trader Alexander McKay and the translator Josechal paddled into shore on a rowboat. Because of their experience in following the Indian customs, they were warmly received by the tribe and even brought into the Nootka Chief's longhouse for the night.[19] Back on the *Tonquin*, Captain Thorn looked out and noticed many Indians in canoes gathering around the ship holding up furs. He wanted this stop to be as efficient as possible so he gave the signal to allow these Indians to climb aboard and start bartering for their furs. Perhaps he had seen or even engaged in some trading while at Fort Astoria, but its likely that Captain Thorn had zero experience in trading with Indians. He didn't observe the standard practice of first presenting gifts of tobacco or other offerings first before the trading began. Additionally, he was not a patient person so when these savvy Indians started a bartering process which could last all day, he became frustrated.

As the day went on, the inexperienced and impatient sea captain cast aside all customs. Instead of bartering, Thorn gave an insultingly low offer for their furs. One of the elder Nootkas rejected Thorn's offer so the captain furiously ripped the furs out of his hands and rubbed them in his face and kicked everyone off the ship.[20] Captain Thorn was convinced this would put the Indians in their place and show them he was the one to be respected, not the other way around. The rest of his crew thought otherwise and urged the defiant captain to pull up anchor and leave immediately. Captain Thorn ignored these warnings and instead retired to his cabin until morning.

Early that next morning, a handful of canoes paddled up to the *Tonquin* and gestured that they intended to trade again. Captain Thorn gave the approval for them to come aboard and quickly a dozen Nootka were on deck. Below, many more canoes were paddling up to the ship bringing even more Indians. Eventually there were several dozen Nootka on the deck of the *Tonquin*. The American crew started getting anxious at the growing number of Indians climbing over the railing but Captain Thorn remained confident that these heathens could do nothing to him or his ship. Eventually too many nervous eyed Nootka were aboard that

19 Stark, *Astoria*, 202.
20 Stark, *Astoria*, 203.

Mark Myers. *Some Evil Design.*
Watercolor on paper, 2001. Courtesy of Mark Myers.

one of the American's signaled to clear the deck. It was too late because at that moment one of the Nootka leaders gave out a shrill cry signaling the rest to remove their fur cloaks and attack. They had not come to trade on this day, they planned to commandeer the ship and kill its crew. Captain Thorn was one of the first to be killed as the Nootka swarmed the ship and got their long-awaited revenge.

A handful of crewmen escaped to safety below deck where they armed themselves and began fighting back. This dispersed the Indians from the *Tonquin* and all fell silent in the cove for the remainder of that day. Later in the night the surviving crewman deliberated on what they should do. A ship of this size required at least twenty men to operate, so it was no longer of use to them. Four of the five survivors chose to escape under the cover of darkness that night by lowering one of the rowboats from the ship and paddling south.

The one remaining survivor aboard the ship was faced with the reality that he would not be taken peacefully. At dawn, dozens of Nootka canoes paddled out to the *Tonquin* and believing it to be deserted, began boarding it. They probably thought they had just acquired a treasure-filled warship, far more valuable than anything they could imagine. But what they didn't account for was the remaining survivor hiding below deck.

According to Joseachal,[21] the Indian translator hired out of Grays Harbor, the *Tonquin* was surrounded by no less than 400 to 500 Indians from the tribe.[22] Then out of nowhere a blinding flash and deafening boom spread out across the water. It is believed that the remaining survivor below deck lit the stockpile of black powder, annihilating everything within the blast radius. It is believed that upwards of 200 Nootka perished in this incredible blast. People are still looking for traces of the *Tonquin* today.[23]

---

21 He had surrendered himself to the tribe as a slave and watched the events unfold from shore. His testimony was the account later used to explain what happened to the "missing" *Tonquin*.

22 Stark, *Astoria*, 215.

23 Since the 1950s, hundreds of thousands of dollars have been spent looking for traces of the ship. In 2003, a crab fisherman snagged on an object that later turned out to be a large 10-foot anchor. This caused a stir among local historians and many believed it might be the actual anchor from the *Tonquin*. It is not certain that it is the actual anchor. See Matthew Preusch, "Tofino, British Columbia." *The New York Times*, September 21, 2003.

The melancholy and fatal catastrophe spread desolation, lamentation, and terror throughout the whole tribe. Scarcely anything belonging to the ship was saved by the Indians, and so terrifying was the effect, so awful the scene, when two other ships passed there soon afterwards, not an Indian would venture to go near them.[24]

A Global Trading Empire Without a Vessel: Fall of 1811

Things could not have turned out worse for the *Tonquin*. Even when we set the tragic human loss aside, losing the *Tonquin* was an enormous setback for the Pacific Fur Company as the ship was a key piece in making the whole operation work. Eventually rumors made their way back to Fort Astoria that something terrible had happened to the ship. Shocking as it may seem, the coastal Indian tribes regularly traded with each other up and down the coast allowing news of this sort to spread by word of mouth.

The sunny weather at Fort Astoria was now fading fast as the winds and rain blew in off the Pacific. This brutal transition that occurs every year is hard for most people in the northwest. Imagine the effects of cold, constant rain beating down on you without the modern luxuries of today let alone those available in 1811.

Just six years earlier when Lewis and Clark wintered just a few miles from the site of Fort Astoria, Lewis had this to say about the weather: "Some rain all day at intervals, we are all wet and disagreeable, as we have been for several days past and our present situation is a very disagreeable one in as much."[25]

As the weather continued to darken, so did the morale. Before long, three Pacific Fur Company employees actually deserted the fort, thinking it better to flee to Spanish settlements in California.[26]

24 Alexander Ross, *Adventures of the First Settlers on the Oregon or Columbia River* (Cleveland: Arthur H. Clark, 1904), 164.

25 Lewis, Meriwether. Clark, William. The Abridgment of the Definitive Nebraska Edition. The Lewis and Clark Journals: An American Epic of Discovery. (University of Nebraska: 2003) 284

26 Stark, *Astoria*, 219.

The three deserters made it as far away as the mouth of the Willamette River, over one hundred miles up the Columbia before being captured by a tribe settled there and returned to an Astorian search party. This was the first time the Astorians had set foot in the fertile Willamette Valley. It was in this special region that the first Masonic lodge in the west would be chartered just thirty six years later.

The Willamette River was first documented by William Clark in April of 1806 after he heard about it from local Indians. At the time, the river was called the "Mult-no-mah"[27] by the local Indians and had a few scattered settlements situated at its mouth (near modern day Portland). Clark found these encampments to be very friendly but complaining of hunger as they were eagerly awaiting the first salmon run of the year.[28] He also heard about a settlement of Indians called the "Cush-hooks" situated at a major waterfall about two days up (the Multnomah) river.[29] Clark and a small party of hunters paddled up the Willamette River to the falls where his family lived. It was around these falls (later became Oregon City, the capital of the Oregon Territory) that Clark saw first hand the destruction of smallpox.

> I observe the wreck of five houses remaining of a very large Village.... I endeavored to obtain from them those people of the Situation of their nation, if scattered or what had become of the natives who must have peopled this great town. An old man who appeared of Some note among them and father to my guide brought forward a woman who was badly marked with the Smallpox and made Signs that they all died with the disorder which marked her face ...from the age of this woman this Di-structive disorder I judge must have been about 28 or thirty years past[30],

27 The first Masonic Lodge West of the Rockies was named Multnomah Lodge and was situated along this same river thirty-six years later.

28 Lewis and Clark Journal, April 2, 1806.

29 These falls were later where John McLoughlin, "Chief Factor" of Hudson Bay Company, established Oregon City which was the home of the first Masonic lodge of Multnomah N⁰ 1.

30 Captain Juan José Pérez Hernández in 1774 on the frigate *Santiago*, followed in 1775 by Captain Bruno de Heceta again on the frigate *Santiago* and Juan Francisco de la Bodega y Quadra captain of the *Señora*, all hailing from Spain. These ships brought widespread destruction to the Indian peoples of the Pacific Northwest who had no prior contact with smallpox and thus no resistance to its devastation.

and about the time the Clatsops inform us that this disorder raged in their towns and distroyed their nation.—Bro. William Clark, April 3, 1806[31]

It is horrifying to think that smallpox knocked out an entire village this far inland and decades before Lewis and Clark's arrival due to contact with European ships. How different American history would be if the Indian populations had been more resistant to European diseases. It is believed that over 180,000 Indians in the region had already died from epidemics by the time Spanish ships arrived in 1774.[32] Prior to that contact, one European ship wrecked along the Pacific coast around 1750 which bore the disease from a Chinese port. This initial outbreak would have been the first of many epidemics to wipe out Native peoples in the region.[33] Later outbreaks would be blamed on fur trappers in the region, among whom the British blamed it on Americans, Americans blamed it on the French and the French in turn on the Spanish.[34]

Life at the Fort: Spring of 1812

The time had come to deliver a message back to Astor in New York City that the Pacific Fur Company was up and running. Once he got word, Astor could send much needed supplies and support. Of course delivering a message to Mr. Astor was no easy feat. The only option the Astorians had was to transport the documents across the continent.[35] It is hard to imagine that anyone was excited to cross the Rockies again after how difficult it had been the first time. However, getting the message to Mr. Astor could make or break the whole company and make all of their prior struggles worth it.[36]

In charge of these two brigades were Mr. Robert Stuart and Mr. John Reed, both partners in the Pacific Fur Company. In April, they reached the thriving village of Wish-ram at the Dalles on the Columbia. It was a custom here for Indians to collect a toll for portaging goods and canoes

---

31 These houses were built of cedar, and were impressive to Lewis and Clark.
32 Patrick Oneill, *The Oregonian*, October 21, 2001, A25.
33 Robert Holmes Ruby & John Arthur Brown, *The Chinook Indians: Traders of the Lower Columbia River* (Norman, Okla.: University of Oklahoma Press, 1976), 34.
34 Ross Cox, *Adventures on the Columbia River* (New York: J. & J. Harper, 1832), 312.
35 The journals were sealed in a tin box strapped to Mr. John Reed's back.
36 Irving, *Astoria*, 2:120.

up or down the rapids.[37] This service was declined because the French voyageurs were already being paid for this very duty. According to journals from Mr. Stuart, there were several hundred Indians "whooping and yelling" around them as the Canadian voyageurs carried the canoes on their shoulders through the village.[38] As the canoes were portaged up the falls, Mr. Stuart and a group stayed back to guard the rest of their belongings.

Tensions mounted between the Astorians and the Indians as a mob surrounded those standing guard. Eventually a small skirmish broke out which caused the Astorians to retaliate with their rifles (killing one of the attackers) who only wielded clubs and tomahawks.[39] In this skirmish Mr. Reed suffered a serious head wound and lost the written letters that were supposed to be delivered to Mr. Astor.

After the chaotic scene had died down and the Indians retreated, the Astorians continued moving their gear up the Dalles and then jumped back in their canoes. As they paddled on, they were unaware that the Indians of which they had just fought off were redoubling their efforts, this time on horseback, and preparing for another attack upriver.[40]

Thankfully the awaiting attackers were spotted and the Astorians pulled their canoes to shore and prepared for another battle. Mr. Reed's head wound was still gushing blood and they discovered he had received five major gashes from a tomahawk.

As they primed their rifles, they were approached by an elderly man in a canoe who communicated that a member of his tribe had been killed and another seriously wounded. It was requested that a member of the Astorians be given over as trade for the slain Indian. This custom of course was unacceptable for the Astorians who instead counter offered a blanket and some tobacco. Amazingly this offer was accepted by the elder and the Astorians were spared any further violence as they advanced up the

37 Or at least stop and offer a parlay. The customs of the white man, being in this case one of haste and economically driven, have always clashed with that of the Indian whose custom it is to sit down and exchange tobacco or series of gifts. When the earlier group of Astorians (David Stuart and Alexander Ross) had passed through the Dalles in July of 1811, they stopped and surrounded by "fearful numbers" of Indians but this incident passed without bloodshed due to their patience in offering a parlay of gifts. They were greatly harassed however by having their goods pilfered through and stolen as they set up camp for the night. See Ross, *Adventures of the First Settlers*, 109–112.

38 Irving, *Astoria*, 2:123.

39 Irving, *Astoria*, 2:127.

40 Irving, *Astoria*, 2:128.

Columbia.[41]

Because the letters they were trying to deliver to Mr. Astor in New York had been stolen, their journey took on a new purpose. The leaders of the group decided to continue heading upriver instead of immediately turning around and going through the same altercation they had just managed to escape. They would paddle another three hundred miles to a post on the Okanogan River where Mr. David Stuart had been stationed since the fall.

To reach this remote location, they would have had to pass through several large Indian nations along the Columbia River. One particular tribe they encountered were the Walla Walla Indians, who were encamped at the mouth of a river with the same name. We have valuable details about this tribe thanks to the journal of Alexander Ross, a Pacific Fur Company clerk who had just passed through it months before.

> The men were generally tall, raw-boned, and well dressed; having all buffalo-robes, deer-skin leggings, very white, and most of them garnished with porcu pine quills. Their shoes were also trimmed and painted red;—altogether, their appearance indicated wealth.
>
> Their voices were strong and masculine, and their language differed from any we had heard before. The women wore garments of well dressed deer-skin down to their heels; many of them richly garnished with beads, higuas, and other trinkets—leggings and shoes similar to those of the men. Their faces were painted red.
>
> On the whole, they differed widely in appearance from the piscatory tribes we had seen along the river. The tribes assembled on the present occasion were the Walla Wallas, the Shaw Haptens, and the Cajouses; forming altogether about fifteen hundred souls. The plains were literally covered with horses, of which there could not have been less than four thousand in sight of the camp.[42]

This proud nation of Walla Walla Indians were friendly and very hospitable to the Astorians. Not only were they hosted to a salmon feast but upon leaving one of their possessions behind accidentally, three Walla Walla Indians returned it to them days later.[43]

41 Irving, *Astoria*, 2:130.
42 Ross, *Adventures of the First Settlers*, 127.
43 Ross, *Adventures of the First Settlers*, 131.

Walla Walla people. Undated photograph.
National Archives and Records Administration.

By the time the Astorians reached Fort Okanogan, they were relieved to find that Mr. David Stuart had stockpiled quite a supply of beaver pelts. For the partners in the Pacific Fur Company, this meant a huge payday to come.

Fort Okanogan

The first American owned settlement in Washington State was this post on the Okanogan River set up by the Pacific Fur Company in the fall of 1811. It was established by partner David Stuart, clerk Alexander Ross, three voyageurs and two Hawaiians. They had paddled far up the Columbia River in order to establish a satellite post that would bring in more pelts from the interior to Fort Astoria.[44]

Why did they pick such a remote location? They needed to be far enough away from the nearest North West Company post that they would be able to compete for the Indian trade. The norm was for a fur company to establish a post near a tribe in order to encourage that tribe into trapping and trading with it. Of course, this only worked until the next fur company beat the deal the first company had set.

The post on the Okanogan River was ultimately chosen because the Indians camped at the mouth of this river actually solicited their services and location as superior to others in the area. This provides an interesting example of a tribe being well aware of the benefits of working with a fur company to improve their living conditions.[45]

Once the location was found, a camp was set up and construction began on a primitive log shelter. With this housing in place, the group again split up with two voyageurs and two Hawaiians heading back downriver to Astoria while Mr. Stuart ventured upriver with a voyageur. This left only the clerk, twenty-nine year old Alexander Ross, in charge of the post. As it was his primary duty to journal all events and transactions at the post, he wrote extensively during this time of isolation. A sense of his extreme paranoia can be felt in the following passage:

> Every day seemed a week, every night a month. I pined, I languished, my head turned gray, and in a brief space ten years were added to my age. Yet man is born to endure, and my only consolation was in my Bible.
>
> Every night before going to bed I primed my gun and pistol anew, and barricaded the door of my lonely dwelling: and the Indians, friendly inclined, always withdrew from the house at dusk; yet they had often alarms among themselves, and often gave me to

44 Under the added protection trader David Thompson and his party who were returning back upriver after finding much to their chagrin that the mouth of the Columbia had already been claimed by Astor's fur company.

45 Ross, *Adventures of the First Settlers*, 142.

understand that enemies, or ill-disposed Indians, were constantly lurking about; and whenever they began to whoop or yell in the night, which they frequently did, I of course partook of the alarm.[46]

Ross' presence in the area attracted a growing encampment of curious Indians that eventually grew to be several hundred in number. Imagine being alone every night, barricaded in a log house surrounded by hundreds of Indians that had never seen anyone like you before.[47]

With Mr. Stuart gone longer than expected, the Indians became wary of the fact that the great trader was missing. Ross tried to persuade them into trapping beavers while he was gone because Mr. Stuart would surely return with many "white man's goods."[48] As it turned out, Mr. Stuart was gone a full six months—and Ross thus alone for six months—trapping and curing an astonishing 1,550 beaver pelts.[49]

Coming Back from Fort Okanogan

When the time came for Mr. Stuart to return, he had between 15-20 bales of furs. On their way back down the Columbia, the Astorians passed two wretched white men yelling at them from shore. It turned out to be two of Hunt's overland party who had been left behind in the Blue Mountains. Through miraculous odds, these two [50] had survived by each others side and thanks to the friendly Walla Walla Indians.[51]

It is hard to imagine the relief these two must have felt when they were able to hail down the canoes of their fellow countrymen. They eagerly climbed aboard the overloaded canoes and held on until they reached Fort Astoria in May of 1812.

Meanwhile at Fort Astoria: May 1812

By now everyone had lost hope that the *Tonquin* would be coming back. Fortunately, an even larger ship named the *Beaver* had been dispatched from New York City thanks to Mr. Astor. Weighing four hundred and

46 Ross, *Adventures of the First Settlers*, 146-47.

47 Ross, *Adventures of the First Settlers*, 148.

48 Ross, *Adventures of the First Settlers*, 150.

49 Ibid.

50 Ramsay Crooks and John Day

51 Irving, *Astoria*, 2:133.

ninety tons, this ship carried one Pacific Fur Company partner by the name of Mr. John Clarke along with five clerks, fifteen American laborers, six Canadian voyageurs and a dozen laborers picked up in Hawaii.[52]

The *Beaver* arrived at the mouth of the Columbia just days before Mr. Stuart's group made it back from Fort Okanogan. One can imagine the boost in morale this must have been for everyone stationed at Fort Astoria as it brought fresh men, new trade goods, and most importantly a new ship.

Efforts were now doubled to spread out and establish new posts on the Columbia. Mr. David Stuart returned upriver to his post on the Okanogan River, his nephew Robert Stuart was again entrusted to deliver documents to Mr. Astor in New York while partners M'Kenzi and Clarke were to establish their own posts. This time, several men were eager to accompany Robert Stuart back to the United States as they were done with this rugged life in the West.

Another Brigade Heads Upriver: June 1812

With their numbers bolstered to around sixty this time, the Astorians embarked on their second attempt up the great Columbia River to deliver documents to Mr. Astor. Paddling a brigade of ten canoes and two barges were the Canadian voyageurs and Hawaiian laborers. When they reached the Dalles, they fortified themselves for the night. Robert Stuart did not want a repeat of the last catastrophe he experienced here several months before. Their weapons were ready and they wore thick elk skin robes that would defend them against arrowheads.[53]

Fortunately their group was large enough to deter the Indians from causing them any trouble. They paddled unharmed onwards to the Walla Walla River where the party of sixty was to split up. Robert Stuart would lead a group back to St. Louis while his uncle David Stuart would take a group to Fort Okanogan and relieve the solitary life of Alexander Ross. An additional group would be led by Mr. M'Kenzie and Mr. Clarke who would set up a fort next door to the Spokane House.[54]

52 Irving, *Astoria*, 2:139.

53 Irving, *Astoria*, 2:146. These leather coats were made by the Columbia River Indians and highly valued by Northern tribes in trade.

54 The Spokane House was established in 1810 by the Canadian Northwest Company about 10 miles downstream of the modern day city of Spokane, Washington. For sixteen years the Spokane House operated as the first long term, non-Indian settle-

Mr. Stuart to St. Louis

Mr. Stuart steered his party through the thick virgin forests of the Blue Mountains[55] and successfully emerged on the (eastern) dry side near modern day La Grande, Oregon. By mid-August they entered the harsh, rocky terrain near the Snake River. One night while camping along the banks of this river, they were approached by a solitary Shoshone Indian. He informed them about a white man who had been living with a nearby settlement. This piqued the interest of the whole party, especially those who had survived the ordeal with Brother Hunt the year before.

The next morning they spurred their horses upriver and inquired about the supposed white man in the area. What they ended up finding was the Shoshone man who had been the guide of Mr. Hunt's party the previous winter. In fact, this was the same one that Hunt had talked into guiding him through the snowy pass to Fort Henry the year before.[56]

After communicating through the broken translations of their interpreter, the Shoshone man agreed to guide them back across the Rocky Mountains, this time by way of a much easier route.[57] Sadly, just a day into this journey, he ran off with Mr. Stuart's best horse in the middle of the night. Frustrated and disheartened, they carried on more vigilant against the approach of "helpful" Indians.

It was late August when they discovered the white men living in the area. It turned out to be John Hoback, Joseph Miller, Jacob Rezner, and Robinson[58] who had been separated from Hunt's overland group 8 months before. These men had been robbed multiple times by Indians and were now found wandering barefoot and bare-chested through the wild.

After being relieved by Mr. Stuart's group, three of these four men

ment in Washington State by essentially becoming the headquarters of the Rocky Mountain fur trade.

55 The Blue Mountains are part of the larger Columbia River Plateau east of the Cascade Range and roughly 300 miles southeast of Portland, Oregon. The highest peaks include the Elkhorn Mountains which are over 9,000 feet in elevation. This range would become the final (land based) obstacle that pioneers had to cross on the Oregon Trail.

56 "Mr. Stuart urged him to accompany them as a guide, promising to reward him with a pistol, with powder and ball, a knife, an awl, some blue beads, a blanket and a looking glass. Such a catalogue of riches was too tempting to be resisted." See Irving, *Astoria*, 2:164.

57 Irving, *Astoria*, 2:162.

58 The man who had been scalped and left for dead years before.

would decide to go off again on their own. The temperament of these trappers is clearly shown through decisions such as this.

Now composed of a party of seven men, Mr. Stuart navigated his way through the forested region of what is now eastern Idaho. Late one night they were awoken by hooping and hollering thundering out of the forest. It was a group of Crow Indians on horseback spooking Mr. Stuart's horses and running off with them in the process. This left the respected partner of the Pacific Fur Company, Robert Stuart, and his men without any horses in the middle of nowhere. To make matters even more concerning, they were entering Blackfoot country.

Wandering Again in the Wilderness: Fall of 1812

Mr. Stuart was well aware of the suffering that Hunt's party had experienced in the region so he pressed on into the Rockies hoping to beat the winter storms. His small group trekked on foot through a wild and dangerous land expending a lot of energy in the process. They were literally living one kill at a time, often going days in between successful hunts.

The plains between the Wyoming and Wind River Mountain Ranges of western Wyoming are no place for man. Even today, this barren landscape is mostly dirt and sagebrush as far as the eye can see. If you were to drive across its fifty mile span, you would only pass through the town of Big Piney, a sprawling metropolis of two hundred homes and five hundred souls as of the 2010 census.[59] To be clear, the combined population of the four nearest towns to Big Piney does not surpass five hundred. But, two centuries ago, this region was very wild and could be filled with game during the right time of year.

As the group made their way out across the vast plain, they hoped they would run into buffalo as they were now in the territory of the great herds. As numerous as buffalo were, they were migratory animals and not just spread out evenly across the countryside. For the first few days the only signs of life were the skeletal remains of buffalo killed long before. Each day they were growing more desperate when finally they spotted an "old run down buffalo bull."[60] One of the hunters of the party successfully brought it down and it was eaten right there on the spot, some of it raw. With their bellies full of lean protein, they would live to see another day.

59 U.S. Census Bureau, 2010 Census.
60 Irving, *Astoria*, 2:209.

The group continued southward and eventually came to a welcome sight: a dozen teepees along the banks of the beautiful New Fork River. These turned out to be Shoshones who welcomed the wary white men into their camp.[61] What Mr. Stuart and his men needed more than anything were horses. The Shoshones were only able to provide one horse (and not an impressive one at that) as they too had recently been robbed by the Crow Indians. Thanks to this one horse, they were able to pack five days' worth of buffalo meat on its back to ensure their survival in the days to come.

It was late October when they reached a large stream they believed was part of the headwaters of the Missouri River. They were partially right, as they stream they had found was actually the headwaters of the Platte River which fed into the Missouri 600 miles to the east. Near this steady and clear stream they began to regularly spot black tailed deer, big horned sheep and large buffalo herds.

Unbeknownst to these seven trail blazers at the time, the very route they were following would later be used by thousands of covered wagons as part of the Oregon Trail. During this journey, famous landmarks like South Pass were discovered through good fortune rather than following a map. Additionally, they had just crossed the continental divide through the famous South Pass, the main passage that thousands of wagons used in crossing the Rockies.

In November, Stuart's group set up a winter camp due to the worsening weather. One morning they were bolted awake by the shrieks of what could only be hostile Indians.

Mr. Stuart walked out of their fort and extended his hand in peace to the chief of the group. Fortunately, this band of Arapaho Indians meant no harm to Stuart or his men but instead asked if they had any food to spare. Mr. Stuart wisely offered some dried buffalo meat to the Indians and they peacefully departed. It was now apparent how vulnerable they were in the middle of nowhere so they packed up and continued moving east.[62]

The group was traveling on foot through what is now central Wyoming in the dead of winter. The average night time temperature for this region in December is one degree Fahrenheit and the average daytime high is

61 Irving, *Astoria*, 2:212.
62 Irving, *Astoria*, 2:238.

Arthur Bierstadt. *The Buffalo Trail.*
Oil on canvas, 1867. Museum of Fine Arts, Boston.

thirty degrees Fahrenheit.[63] To think that they were just delivering letters to Mr. Astor is astonishing. As the days passed, the landscape transformed from forested grassland to a frozen desert and with this their outlook grew dim.

There was no other choice than to just keep putting one foot in front of the other and hoping Providence would deliver them. In late December they reached the Platte River which they had hoped to float down to the Missouri River. Unfortunately, the Platte was completely frozen over so they would have to wait for it to thaw in the spring.

Down the Platte: March 1813

The reader can now imagine a landscape where no evidence of civilization could be seen for as far as the eyes could see. Indeed, Mr. Stuart and his men had not seen a brick building, a road or wagon in over a year and they certainly weren't near any now. They were traveling through one of the purest landscapes ever in North America.

The only traces of human beings they came across were the remnants

63 NOAA National Centers for Environmental Information. "Data Tools: 1981–2010." *https://www.ncdc.noaa.gov/cdo-web/datatools/normals*, accessed February 2, 2017.

of old Indian hunting camps and these were nothing more than fire pits and buffalo bones. The scenery must have been incredible with herds of wild horses and endless buffalo along the banks of the Platte.[64]

One day they met a passing Otoe Indian[65] who informed them about the current war between the United States and England. This was not only their first time hearing about the War of 1812, but also the first intelligence about the United States they had received since they left Fort Astoria in June of the previous year. The Otoe man kindly led Mr. Stuart and his men to his settlement nearby where they were delighted to meet two white traders from St. Louis. Mr. Stuart's group were able to catch up on the latest news from the States but even more importantly they learned that St. Louis was close.

It was now mid-April and the Astorians were somewhere near modern day Omaha, Nebraska on the Platte River. A few days of further paddling and their canoes entered the Missouri River. As eager as they must have been to continue onwards to St. Louis, they decided to stop first at Fort Osage,[66] where they were warmly received by the officers stationed there. Finally, they were able to fill their bellies with fresh baked bread and other culinary delights they had not tasted in over a year.[67]

The winter of 1813 was one of the coldest on record. Stuart journaled about four and a half feet of snow on the ground and the need for snow shoes.[68] As miserable as the cold must have been, the sense of relief of having survived the journey to the Pacific and back to the United States must have been overwhelming. When they finally did stagger back in to St. Louis their presence caused quite a shock as they were the first group

64 Irving, *Astoria*, 2:244.

65 Historically lived along the Missouri River in the Central Plains of Nebraska, Kansas, Iowa and Missouri. The Otoe people were the first Native Americans that Lewis and Clark met on their journey in 1805. They are today federally recognized as the Otoe Tribe of Oklahoma.

66 Fort Osage was located approximately 20 miles downriver from modern day Kansas City, Missouri. It was established in 1808 when Brother William Clark led a team in September to begin construction of the fort. Two months later Brother Pierre Chouteau negotiated the Treaty of Fort Clark with leaders of the Osage Nation to allow its existence in their territory. The fort was abandoned in June of 1813 (two months after Mr. Stuart's visit) due to its troops being needed to fight in the South in the War of 1812. It was reoccupied in 1815. It is today a National Historic Landmark. *http://en.wikipedia.org/wiki/Fort_Osage*.

67 Irving, *Astoria*, 2:249.

68 Stuart & Spaulding, *On the Oregon Trail*, 158.

Marshall Johnson. *Constitution and Guerriere, August 19, 1812.*
Negative on glass, 1912. Library of Congress.

since the Lewis and Clark Corps of Discovery to return from the Pacific.

The War of 1812

The United States declared war on Great Britain on June 18th, 1812, for several reasons. First and foremost, the aim was to bring an end to the practice of British war ships stopping American ships as they left American ports and forcing American sailors into the British Navy. This was known as *impressment*, and was legal under British law and practice up until the end of the Napoleonic Wars in 1814.[69] As many as 10,000 American seamen were impressed into the British Navy to fight against Napoleon.[70] The war was fought on three fronts: at sea on the Atlantic coast, in the Northwest Territory of the United States and on the Gulf Coast.[71]

This relatively short war had lasting impressions on our American way

---

69 Impressment began as a practice under Queen Elizabeth in 1563 and continued under various titles and laws up until the War of 1812.

70 J.C.A. Stagg, *The War of 1812: Conflict for a Continent* (New York: Cambridge University Press, 2012) 128.

71 Not to be confused with the Pacific Northwest. The Northwest Territory of the U.S. was composed in 1812 of the modern states of Ohio, Indiana, Michigan and Wisconsin. This front was mainly fought against the Native American tribes of that region who were being supplied with British weapons.

of life. It gave rise to the leadership of Bro. Andrew Jackson,[72] inspired the writing of "The Star Spangled Banner" by Francis Scott Key, and caused a major shift in the U.S. military, which afterwards became composed of professional enlisted men rather than militia members.

For John Jacob Astor's Pacific Fur Company, this war was especially troubling because it meant everything on the west coast was up for grabs to the British. To make matters worse, he hadn't heard any news since the *Tonquin* left New York and Hunt's overland party left St. Louis. Had the British owned Northwest Company already claimed the mouth of the Columbia by the time the *Tonquin* got there? Had Indians killed or captured Hunt's party? Did the *Tonquin* even make it around the Cape?

Astor's temperament did not allow for inaction in the face of such concerns. He was pragmatic during this period, and even tried to get the U.S. Navy involved in defending Fort Astoria. Still, no matter how convincing he could be, it was hard to justify sending reinforcements to a settlement he could not be sure even existed. It took a full eleven months after the start of the War of 1812 for Astor to definitively hear back from the Pacific Fur Company. Brother Astor read in a newspaper that Mr. Stuart and his handful of men had safely returned to St. Louis.[73] From Astor's perspective, his plan to establish an empire on the Pacific was becoming a reality.

Now that Astor knew for sure that his plans were moving forward, he redoubled his efforts to defend and supply it. He went so far as to request from the Secretary of State, James Monroe, that Navy ships be deployed to the mouth of the Columbia to defend his (and other American) interests there. This request was denied because the war was ramping up on the Great Lakes. U.S. military support was needed on the home front rather than at Astor's private venture 20,000 miles away. This was a blow to Mr. Astor but he did manage to get an official escort by the *U.S.S. Constitution*[74] for his fast moving ship—the *Lark*[75]—as it left the harbor.[76] Additionally, he sent a letter to be delivered to Bro. Hunt which read:

72 Jackson was a member of Greenville Lodge № 119, Greenville, Tennessee. He received the Entered Apprentice degree on May 5, 1851.

73 Irving, *Astoria* 2:295.

74 Stuart & Spaulding, *On the Oregon Trail*, 14.

75 The *Lark* wrecked in a storm off the coast of Hawaii. See Irving, *Astoria* 2:322.

76 Astor did get government support when the U.S.S. *Constitution* escorted the Lark for a few hours out of New York's Harbor. See Kenneth Spaulding, *On the Oregon Trail: Robert Stuart's Journey of Discovery* (Norman, Ok.: 1953), 14.

Aleksandr Olgin. *New Archangle, Sitka, Alaska.*
Pencil and watercolor on paper, 1837. State Archive of the Russian Navy.

Were I on the spot, and had the management of affairs, I would defy them all; but, as it is, everything depends upon you and your friends about you. Our enterprise is grand, and deserves success, and I hope in God it will meet it. If my object was merely gain of money, I should say, think whether it is best to save what we can, and abandon the place; but the very idea is like a dagger to my heart.[77]

Life Goes on at Fort Astoria: August, 1812

After Astor's previous supply ship the *Beaver arrived*, Fort Astoria was doing just fine through the summer of 1812. The men employed at the fort had no knowledge about the war with the British happening back in the States. With life relatively stable, Hunt decided it was time to make connections with the Russian posts in Alaska. This was part of the original plan for the Pacific Fur Company to trade with remote Russian posts in order to obtain their precious otter and seal pelts.

After just a few months of his arrival at Fort Astoria, brother Hunt and a crew of sailors set out on the *Beaver* tacking north for the Gulf of Alaska. For those still stationed at Fort Astoria, this departure meant a considerable reduction in defense and manpower. Hunt reassured everyone

---

77 Irving, *Astoria*, 2:256.

Saint Paul Island, Alaska.
Photo by Bill Briggs. Wikimedia Commons.

that he planned to be back within two months with a cargo hold full of furs. Despite Hunt's confidence in his mission, this would be the last time the Astorians would see the *Beaver*.

Hunt sailed in favorable conditions to New Archangel[78] where he hoped to get off to a good start with the Russian-American Company.[79] In charge of operations here was a man named Alexander Baranov[80] or "Count Baranov" as he was called.[81] Baranov had become rich from the maritime fur trade with the local Kodiak Indians.

78 Modern day Sitka, Alaska. At this settlement only 10 years before occurred a major showdown between the original inhabitants, the Tlingit Indians and the Russian colonizers. First the Tlingit attacked and killed most of the Russians but held Baranov ransom for 10,000 rubles. Two years later Baranov returend with a large army and reclaimed the fort. See Hector Chevigny, *Lord of Alaska: Baranov and the Russian Adventure* (New York: Viking Press, 1942), 320.

79 State sponsored chartered company under Tsar Paul I in 1799, designed to establish new settlements in Russian America (Alaska).

80 Alexander Andreyevich Baranov (1747–1819), chief manager of the Russian American Company. He established the settlement at Sitka Sound in 1799. See Stephen R. Bown, *Merchant Kings: When Companies Ruled the World, 1600–1900* (New York: Thomas Dunne Books, 2010), 154–57.

81 Irving, *Astoria*, 2:304.

It was Hunt's plan to trade Astor's goods from New York City with this rich fur baron. What Hunt didn't prepare for was the lengthy visit that Baranov expected of his guests.

> He is continually giving entertainments by way of parade, and if you do not drink raw rum, and boiling punch as strong as sulphur, he will insult you as soon as he gets drunk, which is very shortly after sitting down at the table.[82]

The Count's excessive drinking delayed Hunt's visit much longer than he had hoped. It took a full forty-five days for the two to make a deal.[83] To make matters worse, none of Baranov's furs were stored on site. Hunt would have to sail 1,000 miles out into the Bering Sea to the Island of St. Paul.[84] By the time he finally made it there, he was supposed to be back at Fort Astoria. Instead, brother Hunt was on a remote Island 2,000 miles out in the middle frigid ocean.

By November, the *Beaver* was loaded with pelts but winter conditions were setting in. One night a heavy storm came through and thrashed the rudder of the ship. The damage was so severe that it dissolved all hope of returning to Fort Astoria that year. Instead Hunt would have to winter in Honolulu and charter a different ship back to the Columbia River in the Spring. This plan was again doomed with bad luck.

Hunt ended up stranded in Honolulu until the following summer waiting for the first American ship, the *Albatross*, to come into port. He chartered the *Albatross* for $2,000[85] which brought him back to Fort Astoria in August of 1813, exactly one year after he had left.

Fort Astoria Lacks Loyalty and Leadership: January of 1813

Left in charge of the fort after Hunt's departure was another PFC partner named Duncan M'Dougal. M'Dougal was a Scotsman who had previously worked for the North West Company. Not only did he have to manage his employees but he also had to stay on friendly terms with the estimated 1,000 local Indians of the Chinook, Clatsop, Tillamook and Chelais

82 Irving, *Astoria*, 2:306.

83 Irving, *Astoria*, 2:309.

84 Kenneth Wiggins Porter, *John Jacob Astor* (Cambridge, Mass.: Harvard University Press, 1931), 1:206-207.

85 Irving, *Astoria*, 2:315.

tribes.[86] Little excitement happened around the fort until January of 1813, when Mr. M'Kenzie returned disgruntled from his post up the Columbia.[87]

While at his post near the Spokane House, M'Kenzie heard from a Mr. John M'Tavish[88] of the North West Company that America was at war with Britain. Being that the North West Company was British and the Pacific Fur Company was American, the two competing trading companies were now in an entirely new situation. More troubling was when M'Kenzie heard that an armed ship by the name of the *Isaac Todd* was on its way to obtain the post at the mouth of the Columbia.[89]

How quickly fortunes changed in the wild west. All the labor put in to starting Fort Astoria would soon be lost. Had the *Tonquin* and its crew not been destroyed, perhaps it would have been able to fight off the *Isaac Todd*. Instead, civilian employees at the fort would have had to fight for their lives using a few cannons and rifles against a full on battleship. Additionally, Fort Astoria's leader M'Dougal had no desire to fight his former countrymen and employer. It would be much easier for him to just go back to working for the NWC when they arrived. So in anticipation of the arrival of the *Isaac Todd*, M'Kenzie and M'Dougal agreed to suspend all trade with local Indians and secretly made plans to sell off all stock to the North West Company.[90]

Being that there was only one way to relay a message to the other partners at Fort Okanogan and Spokane, M'Kenzie again went upriver to inform Mr. Stuart and Mr. Clarke of the bad news. To reach these remote posts, M'Kenzie joined seventeen voyageurs in a pair of canoes who paddled him back up the Columbia River. After reaching the Dalles, M'Kenzie met up with a brigade of white men paddling downstream. It turned out to be none other than Mr. John M'Tavish himself on his way to rendezvous with the *Isaac Todd*. Both parties went their separate ways after spending an evening together camped on the banks of the Columbia.

---

86 214 Chinooks, 180 Clatsops, 234 Chehalis and 200 TIllamooks. See Ruby & Brown, *The Chinook Indians*, 133.

87 Irving, *Astoria*, 2:271.

88 At thirty-five years of age, John George McTavish started out as a clerk in Montreal working for the NWC. He was eventually promoted to a partner in the company and had been one for just a year by the time he negotiated the deal with M'Dougal to acquire the Pacific Fur Company holdings. *http://www.biographi.ca/en/bio/mctavish_john_george_7E.html*.

89 Irving, *Astoria*, 2:273.

90 Irving, *Astoria*, 2:274.

When M'Kenzie finally reached Mr. Stuart at Fort Okanogan and Mr. Clarke at Fort Spokane, both partners were outraged at the news. They couldn't believe that he and M'Dougal wanted to sell to the NWC.

> If their trip upriver was just around the bend or a days paddle it would be understandable, but they had to paddle over 400 miles upriver to Mr. Clarke at Fort Spokane and from thence another 150 miles to Mr. Stuart at Fort Okanogan. Once M'Kenzie delivered the bad news to the two posts, the voyageurs had to paddle another 500 miles back down the Columbia: a one thousand-mile round-trip in the matter of a month.

Despite the horrible news, both Mr. Stuart and Mr. Clarke decided to not immediately return to Fort Astoria. Instead, they remained at their posts to continue stockpiling furs. They waited until the date they had previously agreed upon to rendezvous at the mouth of the Walla Walla River. Here they met up with M'Kenzie and his crew of voyageurs. The three partners along with their crews now joined forces as one large brigade with six canoes and two barges loaded with bales of furs.[91] By the time they made it to Fort Astoria on June 12, 1813[92] all their furs would end up being sold to the North West Company at one third of their true value.[93]

Arguments at the Fort: Summer 1813

M'Dougal was well underway preparing to sell off the fort to the North West Company by the time Mr. Stuart and Clarke arrived. As they all were equal partners in the Pacific Fur Company, tempers flared about just giving up after so much had been already invested. By now Hunt had been absent for nearly a year and so the partners came to an agreement without him.[94] The Pacific Fur Company had been operating at Fort Astoria for two years, but the threat of an approaching British warship diminished all hope that it could hold out.

---

91 Furs were pressed into bales which were tightly strapped together and wrapped into bales. The standard weight of a bale was 90 lbs.

92 Irving, *Astoria*, 2:284.

93 Irving, *Astoria*, 2:332.

94 Irving, *Astoria*, 1:291.

Reluctantly, a manifesto was signed and sent via the North West Company express to Mr. Astor in New York.[95]

With the Astorians' supply of trade goods now dwindling, the Chinook Indians grew frustrated that there was nothing left to trade for their furs. This strained the relationship between the two groups. To keep Chief Comcomly happy, M'Dougal married one of the elder's daughters.[96] This improved relations between the Astorians and the Chinook for a time. All was going according to plan for M'Dougal until a ship appeared at the mouth of the Columbia flying an American flag. It was brother Hunt aboard the *Albatross* returning from his whirlwind tour of the Pacific.

Hunt Makes a Brief Stop at Astoria: August 1813

A lot had changed at Fort Astoria in the year Hunt had been gone. As a result of the fact that everything was being sold to the NWC, Hunt ended up just staying for six days. Surely those first few days he spent arguing with the other partners about the sale of their company. The later days were spent stockpiling the albatross with furs and preparing to return twenty-five Hawaiian laborers to their native paradise.[97] Before returning to Hawaii, the *Albatross* had other business to attend to in the Marquesas Islands. While in port for this layover, brother Hunt met the famed Navy Captain, David Porter. Captain Porter informed Hunt about several British warships assumed to be headed for the Columbia: the *Phoebe*, *Racoon* and *Cherub*.

Hunt was desperate to get back to Fort Astoria to notify his partners but no matter how determined he was, there was no way he could charter an American ship due to the War of 1812. Reluctantly, Hunt would have to sail back to Hawaii aboard the *Albatross* and from thence take another ship back to the Columbia River.

He finally made it back to Hawaii in December where he learned about the fate of yet another Astorian ship: the *Lark*. It had wrecked just off of the Hawaiian Islands, joining the *Tonquin* at the bottom of the sea.

---

95 At this time the express was likely a series of canoe and horse portages from the Columbia River to Fort William on Lake Superior. This route later became the York Factory express used by the Hudson's Bay Company. See Richard S. Mackie, *Trading Beyond the Mountains: The British Fur Trade on the Pacific, 1793-1843* (Vancouver, B.C.: University of British Columbia Press, 1997), 16.

96 Irving, *Astoria*, 2:297.

97 Irving, *Astoria*, 2:319.

As a result of this turn of events, Hunt chartered another ship called the *Pedlar*, putting the captain of the *Lark* at its wheel and headed back to Fort Astoria on January 22, 1814.[98]

To Take and Destroy Everything American on the Northwest Coast: October 1813

It was only a month after Hunt left Fort Astoria that it officially changed hands over to the North West Company. With a brigade of seventy-five men aboard ten canoes, Mr. M'Tavish partner of the North West Company, arrived at Fort Astoria for the second time in 1813. This visit was different in that he was there to obtain the properties of the Pacific Fur Company.

For the American employees living at the Fort, it was unbelievable to watch everything they had worked so hard for be signed over to another company.[99] The North West Company was now in charge of not only the fort but the entire Columbia River territory. The day would soon come when the American Flag was lowered and replaced by the Union Jack, officially starting the tug of war between the U.S. and Great Britain for the region.

To help rationalize his decision to sell, M'Dougal assembled the Pacific Fur Company employees and read to them a letter he had received from the North West Company indicating that the *Phoebe* and *Isaac Todd* were in fact on their way to Astoria to "take and destroy everything American on the Northwest coast."[100] With this threat approaching, arrangements were made between M'Dougal and M'Tavish to sell off all of the furs in possession of the Pacific Fur Company. The price settled for ended up being a seventy-five percent loss to the Astorians,[101] a huge hit to their efforts over the past three years. Fortunately for the employees the terms set originally by the Pacific Fur Company were honored and all were compensated fairly. Additionally, PFC employees were able to switch companies if they desired to work under the NWC.

Even in 1813, centuries before corporate takeovers would be the norm

98 Irving, *Astoria*, 2:326.

99 Of which only a fraction were truly American-born.

100 Irving, *Astoria*, 2:329.

101 Furs in stock at Fort Astoria at the time of its sale: 550 beaver, 900 river otter, sixty sea otter, 170 mink, 100 fox, 70 black bear, 15 brown bear. See Irving, *Astoria*, 2:332. Astor took a loss of $160,000 from his initial investment of $500,000. See Dorothy Johansen, *Empire of the Columbia* (New York: Harper & Row, 1967), 105.

in big business, these two companies would arrange the first corporate takeover on the west coast, offering options such as severance packages, travel arrangements, and back pay. Considering the fort could have been seized by armed takeover, it is fortunate that the PFC made any money at all. But for Brother Astor back in New York City whose personal fortunes were tied up in the PFC, he was "disgraced"[102] and never forgave M'Dougal.

The Racoon Arrives Seeking Fortune: November 1813

A state of restlessness hung over Fort Astoria until it peaked on the 30th of November. On this day a new ship was spotted outside of the Columbia bar and turned out to be a British warship but not one they anticipated. It was the *Racoon*,[103] under command of Captain William Black who along with his crew of 120 men were ready to claim the region under the British flag. As it turned out, no American property was to be found when they entered the Columbia River—everything was now owned by the North West Company.

On the 12th of December, after waiting for conditions to become suitable to cross the dreaded sandbar of the Columbia, the *Racoon* dropped anchor off shore of Fort Astoria. Captain Black was paddled into shore where he walked up the rocky bank to the fort. To mark this significant day, he smashed a bottle of wine and christened the fort in honor of a distant King. The first American colony on the west coast was no more, it was now British owned and officially called Fort George.

Within just days of this auspicious event, M'Dougal became a full-fledged partner of the North West Company. He was sure to make a large profit off of the deal he had just made months before with M'Tavish. A few months later in late February, Bro. Hunt returned to the mouth of the Columbia. One can only imagine his feelings upon first seeing the Union Jack flying over the fort. After all of the thousands of miles he had traveled by land and sea, he now had to accept that he had done too little, too late. The only thing he could do now was pack up what documents he could at the fort and leave this dreaded venture in the West never to return.[104]

102 Irving, *Astoria*, 2:334.

103 An eighteen-gun sloop of the Royal Navy launched in 1808. See James Joseph Colledge, *Ships of the Royal Navy* (Annapolis, Md.: Naval Institute Press, 1987), 350.

104 Hunt returned to his native town of St. Louis in 1817, where he settled down and became postmaster.

The Final Overland Journey of the Astorians: April 1814

For the rest of the PFC employees, it was time to decide whether they wanted to enlist with the NWC or return to life in the United States. For those who chose to return to the States they would have to board the *Pedlar* and travel back around the Cape or cross the continent on horseback. Mr. Clarke, M'Kenzie and Stuart all opted for the latter and set off once again up the Columbia River aboard their Chinook canoes. A half dozen or so employees ended up working for the NWC and eventually settled in Willamette Valley, Oregon.[105] Our dear Brother Hunt sailed around the Pacific for a few years, the pure merchant that he was, before returning to New York City in October of 1816.[106]

A notable coincidence occurred as Clarke, M'Kenzie, and Stuart were leaving the Columbia River territory. A voice was heard yelling from shore as they approached the mouth of the Walla Walla River. It turned out to be Marie Dorion, the lone Indian woman who had accompanied Hunt's party across the continent years before. She had been living near the Snake River with partner Mr. Reed since the summer before when everyone except herself and two sons had been killed by Bannock Indians. Through her incredible grit, she survived by living on her own in the wilderness and under the care of the Walla Walla tribe.[107] After a brief reunion, the PFC partners continued onwards to St. Louis while Marie Dorion went to settle in the Willamette Valley where she lived a long life before passing away at the age of sixty-four.[108]

105 J. Neilson Barry, "Astorians Who Became Permanent Settlers." *The Washington Historical Quarterly* 24 (1933): 221-31.

106 Kenneth W. Porter, "Cruise of Astor's Brig Pedler, 1813–1816." *Oregon Historical Quarterly 31* (1930), 223-30.

107 When she died in 1850 her body was buried inside the original log Catholic church in St. Louis, MO. Gayle Shirley, *More Than Petticoats: Remarkable Oregon Women* (Guilford, Conn.: Globe Pequot Press, 2010), 10–13.

108 J. Neilson Barry, "Madame Dorion of the Astorians." *Oregon Historical Quarterly* thirty (1929): 272–78.

1822 *to* 1840

The Mountain
Man Era

THE ERA OF THE MOUNTAIN MAN was ushered in by a small ad placed in the *Missouri Gazette & Public Advertiser* on February 13, 1822, which read:

To enterprising young men. The subscriber wishes to engage ONE HUNDRED MEN to ascend the Missouri River to its source, there to be employed for one, two, or three years-For the particulars enquire of Major Andrew Henry, near the lead mines in the county of Washington, (who will ascend with, and command the party) or to the subscriber near St. Louis.[1]

Brother Andrew Henry
St. Louis Lodge No. 111, St. Louis, Missouri

He was highly respected for his intelligence, enterprise, daring, and honesty…because of his adventurous exploits he figures largely in the early annals of the frontier, and no trapper of his time, with the possible exception of John Colter, had a wider renown as a hero.[2]

Brother Henry entered the fur business in 1809 as a partner in the Missouri Fur Company. Two of the other ten partners in the company were also well known Freemasons: Brothers William Clark and Pierre Chouteau. This company's plans were grand: they hoped to set up trading posts among the various Indian tribes of the upper Missouri River. A partner would be left in charge of each of the forts and supported by at least a dozen enlisted men.

The first expedition of the Missouri Fur Company departed in the spring of 1809 with a massive crew of 350 men and over a dozen keelboats.[3] Brother Henry split off with a group of trappers and attempted to build a fort at modern day Three Forks, Montana. This site was soon abandoned

---

1 Dale L. Morgan, *The West of William H. Ashley* (Denver: The Old West Publishing Company, 1964), 1.

2 Allen Johnson, Dumas Malone, *& Harris Elwood Starr, Dictionary of American Biography* (New York, Charles Scribner's Sons, 1928). 8:546–47.

3 Richard E. Oglesby *& Lisa Manuel, The Opening of the Missouri Fur Trade* (Norman, Okla.: University of Oklahoma Press, 1963), 75.

due to attacks from Blackfoot Indians. Henry and his men fled for their lives into modern day Idaho where they built a string of forts on what is now called Henry's Fork on the Snake River. Even though they were safe from Indian attacks, Henry's men struggled to survive due to the lack of supplies and available food. As a result, they returned east of the Rocky Mountains in the spring of 1811 with valuable experience but crushed hopes. Brother Henry essentially dropped out of the Missouri Fur Company after this to manage his own affairs and had little to do with the industry for the next decade.

Eleven years later in 1822, Henry partnered with William Ashley and outfitted their own company of 100 men to begin trapping beaver in the Montana, Wyoming and Idaho region. Ashley would manage the business side in St. Louis and brother Henry lead his final brigade into the West before retiring. In his ranks were the adventurous young men who had come forward in response to the ad placed in the newspaper.

This was no summer job these young men were applying for. They were enlisting to serve up to three years in the Wild West and many never returned at all. Of those who did make it back, some were forever scarred by their experiences and very few made any money in it. Consider the example of Hugh Glass, a trapper that was savagely attacked by a mother grizzly while hunting on the Grand River in what is now South Dakota.[4] His story of survival has been told in many books and recently brought to life by Leonardo Di Caprio in *The Revenant*.

In the two years that the Ashley-Henry fur company existed, the blue prints were drawn up on what would become the lucrative and wildly exciting Rocky Mountain fur trade. For the Indian tribes who lived west of the Missouri River, this period would mark the beginning of the end to their traditional ways of life. The streams of the Rocky Mountains were simply too populated with beavers to stop these enterprising young men.

While we call them "mountain men," most who entered the trade were actually in their late teens or early twenties. These were the same guys who today would be working as a checker at the grocery store or busing tables at a restaurant. Instead, their first job and taste of the real world

---

4   Rufus B. Sage, *Scenes in the Rocky Mountains: And in Oregon, California, New Mexico, Texas, and the Grand Prairies : Or, Notes by the Way, During an Excursion of Three Years, with a Description of the Countries Passed Through, Including Their Geography, Geology, Resources, Present Condition, and the Different Nations Inhabiting Them* (Philadelphia: Carey & Hart, 1846), 118–22.

was to go out into the Wild West where there was a real danger of being ripped apart by an 800-pound grizzly bear or having their scalp ripped off by an Indian. Clearly these risks were weighed against the rewards to be found in the Rocky Mountain fur trade.

The Annual Rendezvous

When Henry retired in 1825, Ashley decided to double down on his efforts to tap into the Rocky Mountain fur trade. Rather than doing annual trips up the Missouri River with his 100 men, Ashley reconfigured the business to have his men stay in the mountains year round while he and a smaller party would go back and forth from St. Louis for supplies. His 100 enlisted men adapted quite well to this change by splitting up into small groups and then rendezvousing in the summer to sell off their pelts for supplies, whiskey and food.

On July 1, 1825, the first annual rendezvous of mountain men took place just north of modern day McKinnon, Wyoming.[5] At this first gathering, Mr. Ashley must have been very pleased watching his men trickle in from the surrounding wilderness with their horses loaded with pelts. Ashley then delivered these pelt packs back to St. Louis where he sold them to merchants who in turn sold them in New York, China, and London. The value of this first haul was $50,000—over $1,000,000 in modern money.[6]

This rendezvous system would repeat every summer from 1825 to 1840 at various sites across modern day Wyoming, Utah, and Idaho. The sites were selected based on their ability to accommodate large groups of people for weeks at a time and their accessibility to supply trains from St. Louis.[7]

Imagine several hundred bearded mountain men clad in leathers, Indian teepees from various tribes scattered about and a strong buzz

5 Fred Gowans, *Rocky Mountain Rendezvous: A History of the Fur Trade Rendezvous, 1825–1840* (Provo, Utah: Brigham Young University Press, 1975), 18.

6 Dolin, *Fur, Fortune, and Empire*, 226.

7 Supply trains of man powered keel boats and horses. Not to be confused with locomotives which came much later. The first covered wagons to cross the Rocky Mountains occurred in 1830, when a fur company sent ten supply wagons to a rendezvous. It would not be for another decade that emigrants started to use the same method to transport their goods to Oregon Country. See William E. Hill, *The Oregon Trail Yesterday and Today* (Caldwell, Idaho: The Caxton Printers, 1992), 11.

of excitement. Of course, no rendezvous was complete without high powered grain alcohol brought in to replenish the weary mountain men and trade with Indians.

Mr. Ashley's rendezvous system became so successful that he sold his interests in the company after just two years and went into politics. In his second year, Ashely accumulated 125 pelt packs which were sold in St. Louis for $60,000[8] or $1.2 million[9] in today's money. The new partners of the Rocky Mountain Fur Company after 1826 were mountain men themselves: Jedediah Smith, David Jackson and William Sublette. As long as men's fashion demanded top quality beaver felt top hats, mountain men would be wading through icy streams in the Wild West.

> Mirth, songs, dancing, shouting, trading, running, jumping, singing, racing, target shooting, yarns, frolic, with all sorts of extravagances that white men or Indians could invent, were frequently indulged in. The unpacking of the medicine water contributed not a little to the heightening of our festivities.[10]

> The rendezvous is one continued scene of drunkenness, gambling, and brawling and fighting, as long as the money and credit of the trappers lasts…the stakes are "beaver," which here is the coin; and when the fur is gone, their horses, mules, rifles, and shirts, hunting-packs, and breeches are staked. Daring gamblers make the rounds of the camp, challenging each other to play for the trapper's highest stake-his horse, his squaw (if he had one). A trapper often squanders the produce of his hunt, amounting to hundreds of dollars, in a couple hours; and, supplied on credit with another supplier, leaves the rendezvous for another expedition, which has the same result time after time.[11]

The temperament of a mountain man could be compared to a modern day crab fisherman in Alaska. Both jobs attract the same type of individual willing to put himself in danger for a big payday. As tough as

---

8   Dolin, *Fur, Fortune, and Empire*, 226.

9   *http://www.westegg.com/inflation/infl.cgi.*

10   Thomas D. Bonner, *The Life and Adventures of James P. Beckwourth* (New York: Alfred A. Knopf, 1931), 107.

11   George Frederick Augustus Ruxton, *Adventures in Mexico and the Rocky Mountains* (New York : Harper & Brothers, 1848), 236.

David Wright. *Bent's Fort Arrival*. Oil on Panel. Jackson, Wyoming.

both of these jobs are, the dangers of taking an arrow through the rib cage or being eaten alive by a grizzly were very real for mountain men. These were not just rare encounters, they were very real dangers for a mountain man. Nonetheless when it came to reckless young men, all it took was one look at a brigade strolling back into St. Louis with a fortune in furs and they were all in.

Most of these mountain men signed up with a fur company with hopes of coming back from the mountains as rich men but some were simply looking for adventure. "I wanted to be the first to view a country on which the eyes of a white man had never gazed and to follow the course of rivers that run through a new land,"[12] said Jedediah Smith, who survived a grizzly attack but was later killed by Comanche Indians. Before his death in 1831, Smith's adventurous spirit drove him to travel as far west as the Pueblo de Los Angeles[13] and as far north as Fort Vancouver,[14] earning him rank among America's "greatest explorers."[15]

In exchange for rolling the dice with their lives, mountain men were able to see the West as the Great Architect originally designed it. From vast bison herds that shook the earth to endless starry canopies, it was as rich an environment as you might find today in Africa. Unfortunately, within a few generations, the magic of this wild land would vanish. Fortunately for us today we have the imagery from authors and artists who captured the era which otherwise might have been lost forever.

> There is perhaps no class of men on the face of the earth, who lead a life of more continued exertion, peril and excitement, or are more enamored of their occupation, than the free trappers of the West… the wild, Robin Hood kind of life, with all its strange and motley populace, now existing in full vigor in the Rocky Mountains."—Washington Irving's classic, *The Adventures of Captain Bonneville, or scenes beyond the Rocky Mountains of the Far West*[16]

With so many adventurous and enterprising young men seeking a new life in the far west, it is not surprising that some became heroes in their own right. Amongst the drunken brawls, gambling and all around debauchery associated with the annual rendezvous, there was at least

---

12 Robert M. Utley, *A Life Wild and Perilous: Mountain Men and the Paths to the Pacific* (New York: Henry Holt & Co., 1997), 90.

13 Dolin, *Fur, Fortune, and Empire*, 226.

14 Dolin, *Fur, Fortune, and Empire*, 238.

15 William H. Goetzmann, *Exploration and Empire; the Explorer and the Scientist in the Winning of the American West* (New York : Knopf, 1966), 112.

16 Washington Irving, *Adventures of Captain Bonneville, or Scenes Beyond the Rocky Mountains of the Far West* (London: R. Bentley, 1837), 1:13.

Christopher (Kit) Carson, taken between 1860 and 1875.
The Brady-Handy Photograph Collection, Library of Congress.

one man who stood out due to his calm, sober disposition. He was described by some as being "loyal, honest and kind" even "lovable,"[17] yet behind the barrel of a rifle he was a killer. This man was Brother Christopher "Kit" Carson and his travels were as legendary as they come.

Brother Christopher Kit Carson
Montezuma Lodge No. 109, Taos, New Mexico

As a boy, Kit grew up playing with his 9 siblings on a large piece of property called "Boones Lick" in Missouri. At the time (1810-1820), this region was the edge of the American frontier[18] and where the wild west began. At any time during his childhood, there was a real danger that he, his family members or his neighbors would be captured or killed by local

17 Hampton Sides, "Blood and Thunder." *Anchor*, October 9, 2007: 9.
18 Kit was raised on a piece of property called Boone's Lick, about thirty miles west of modern day Columbia, Missouri. This property was named after the sons of Brother Daniel Boone, who purchased the property initially.

Taos Pueblo. Library of Congress.

"The trail to Santa Fe was like a long rope flung carelessly across the plains—an old rope, loosely twisted, so that here and there the strands parted, only to join again…"—Stanley Vestal, *The Old Santa Fe Trail* (University of Nebraska Press, 1939, p. 31

Indians as they went about their day. Yet as could be said about people in any environment, a dichotomy existed where some were friendly and some were not. Young Kit was said to have been friends with children from the local Sac and Fox tribes.[19]

By the time Kit was fourteen he had given up on school and was ready to start earning money for himself. He became an apprentice for a leather man in hopes of learning a trade but became restless with the monotony. Before long he started seeing fur traders coming back on the Santa Fe trail.[20] It was around this time that men were just starting to trickle back into the States from the Mexican South West loaded with furs and stories to boot. Apparently destined to meet the young

19 Sides, "Blood and Thunder," 12.
20 The virtual commencement of the Santa Fe Trail occurred in 1822, when Captain William Becknell took wagons filled with trade goods into the Mexican territory. He was backed by investors in Missouri and had between $25,000 and $30,000 worth of merchandise. See Josiah Gregg, *Commerce of the Prairies* (New York: Henry G. Langley, 1844), 1:10.

and impressionable Kit, these trappers brought their worn out straps and saddles to the shop he worked in and, before long, Kit decided he would rather ride in a saddle than fix one.

In 1826 at the ripe age of sixteen, Kit joined a caravan of traders heading west to Santa Fe. Kit's life from this moment would be one adventure after another in his quest to "see foreign countries."[21]

When Kit arrived in Santa Fe with his caravan, he went on to a nearby town called Taos which was at the time the main hub of the southwestern fur trade.[22] Due to its proximity to the southern Rockies, Taos essentially became a year round rendezvous town for trappers. It was here that Carson met many mountain men, most notably Mathew Kinkhead who was friends with Kit's father back in Missouri.[23] Again Kit became an apprentice, this time for a seasoned trapper and frontiersman.

Even though he was illiterate, Kit started picking up on the local Spanish and Indian dialects which would be crucial in this new environment. He was so savvy that within two years he was hired on as a cook and later as a Spanish translator for a caravan heading south to Chihuahua City, Mexico.

A year later in 1829, at the age of nineteen, Kit was hired on by another mountain man named Ewing Young (1799–1841)[24] to accompany him deep into what was then Apache Indian territory (now central Arizona[25]). Mr. Young was at the time the most accomplished and prominent fur trapper in the Southwest.[26] Interestingly enough, he had arrived in New Mexico a young man himself only seven years before to work as a carpenter.

Seeing the lucrative opportunity available in furs, Young entered a partnership with a man named William Wolfskill. The two found great success trapping in what was Mexican territory on the Gila River. Despite hostilities with Apache Indians and illegally trapping on Mexican land,

21 Christopher Carson, *Kit Carson's Autobiography*, Edited by Milo Milton Quaife (Lincoln: University of Nebraska Press, 1966), 5.

22 Sides, "Blood and Thunder," 17.

23 Ibid.

24 Young later settled in the Willamette Valley, Oregon. He is believed by some to be the first American to build a house on the HBC side of the Willamette River. See John A. Hussey, *Champoeg: Place of Transition, A Disputed History* (Portland: Oregon Historical Society, 1967), 73–74.

25 Sides, "Blood and Thunder," 18.

26 Utley, *A Life Wild and Perilous*, 104.

Young tapped into rich beaver populations and made huge profits.

It was on a similar trip in August of 1829, that the young greenhorn, Kit Carson, demonstrated his value on a fur brigade. Thanks to his steady nerves and natural instincts, Kit easily transitioned into the life of a trapper.

On his first test, Kit was camped with the forty man brigade along the Salt River[27] when the group was attacked by a band of Apaches. After a poorly executed attack, Carson recalled that the trappers had "killed 15 or 20 warriors with a great number wounded"[28] and at least one was shot by Carson.[29]

Fortunately for the trappers, no one in their brigade was killed on this trip. However this attack was only the first of many from Indians. The trappers had to be on guard at all times because if they weren't being out-rightly attacked they were being robbed. Late one night, Apaches stole a bunch of gear and mules which caused the group to split in half, twenty returned to Taos while the other twenty continued trapping.[30]

Even with his brigade at half strength, Young decided to head further west through some of the hottest and most desolate terrain in North America. They were near modern day Flagstaff, Arizona on the headwaters of the Verde River and would be traveling across the Mohave Desert which averages in the mid 90s in late summer.[31] Carson said the land was "burned up…not a drop of water" and they "suffered greatly" during their trek across this scorched earth.[32] Finally, they made it to the Colorado River where they re-hydrated for their journey further into the West.

Fall of 1829, Mohave Desert to Los Angeles

Mr. Young, Brother Kit and the rest of the trappers were now 500 miles west of Taos but only 200 miles east of the California Coast. What an incredible distance they had already covered yet they had only just begun. From the Colorado River, they continued southwest eventually passing through

---

27 A river that flows through modern day Phoenix, AZ

28 Harvey Lewis Carter, *Dear Old Kit: The Historical Christopher Carson* (Norman, Okla.: University of Oklahoma Press, 1926), 44.

29 Stanley Vestal, *Kit Carson: The Happy Warrior of the Old West* (New York, Houghton Mifflin Co., 1928), 47.

30 Utley, *A Life Wild and Perilous*, 110.

31 *http://www.wrcc.dri.edu/cgi-bin/cliMAIN.pl?azking.*

32 Utley, *A Life Wild and Perilous*, 111.

Camp scene in the Mohave Valley of Rio, Colorado.
Color lithograph by T. Sinclair and A. Hoen. Library of Congress.

the San Gabriel Mountains. The brigade would use the same Cajon Pass that today is used by tens of thousands of vehicles via Interstate 15. How dumbfounded these trappers would be if they could see our world today.

Once through the Cajon Pass, they entered an interesting environment characterized by flowering cactus and ten thousand foot mountains. It was the sublime landscape of southern California in its original form. They stayed close to the mountains heading towards the thriving Mission of San Gabriel where they would rest for the winter.[33]

Mission of San Gabriel

On September 8, 1771, the mission was formally founded and dedicated to the Archangel Gabriel. Five years later, across the continent, the *Declaration of Independence* was written. Its goal was to Christianize and naturalize the local Indians as Spanish citizens. Like John McLoughlin at Fort Vancouver, the Mission of San Gabriel was managed by a man of endless energy named Padre Zalvidea. In addition to delivering the word of God to the Indians, Zalvidea ensured they were taught a trade.

33 Ibid.

Ferdinand Deppe. *Mission San Gabriel.*
Oil on canvas, c. 1850. Boston Atheneum.

There were "soap makers, tanners, shoemakers, carpenters, black-smiths, bakers, fishermen, brick and tile makers, cart makers, weavers, deer hunters, saddle makers, shepherds and vaqueros. Large soap works were erected, tannery yards established, tallow works, cooper, blacksmith, carpenter and other shops, all in operation. Large spinning rooms, where might be seen 50 or 60 women turning their spindles and there were looms for weaving wool, cotton and flax. Storehouses filled with grain, and ware houses of manufactured products testified to the industry of the Indians."[34] The Mission San Gabriel became the largest manufacturing center in California for a time.[35]

Spring 1830, Los Angeles to San Francisco

From the picturesque Mission, Young led his brigade north into the San

34 J.M. Guinn, *Historical and Biographical Record of Southern California* (Chicago: Chapman Pub. Co., 1902), 41.

35 Ibid.

Joaquin Valley. They went as far north as modern day Redding, California trapping along the Sacramento River.[36] The farther they went north the more dismayed they became due to a peculiar absence of beavers. Finally they discovered the reason when they crossed paths with another huge brigade three times their size.[37] It turned out to be trappers from the Hudson's Bay Company led by Peter Skene Ogden. Here in the middle of Alta, California, we find two opposing companies trapping illegally yet doing so without any real opposition from the Mexican authorities. This situation would foreshadow what was to come for California in the next few decades.[38]

As summer arrived, Young made it to the tiny village of Yerba Buena, better known today as San Francisco where he hoped to sell off his furs to American ships. Upon reaching the tiny town, Young needed to earn a favor for unloading what were effectively Mexican furs onto an American ship. What better way is there to earn a favor than by doing someone a favor?

At the southern end of San Francisco Bay was the thriving Mission of San Jose.[39] One of its main efforts was to Christianize local Indians who were in actuality several different tribes of very diverse traits. There were the Yokuts or Mariposas, the Miwok and the Wintu peoples who lived in the immediate area.[40] All were attracted to the abundance of food, shelter and comfort available at the mission. However, the mission was plagued with ongoing problems with Indians which peaked right around the time Young's brigade arrived. After a significant riot broke out at the Mission, the Indians fled back into their local settlements. The Mission had no defense and Mexican officials in the area were unable to do anything to punish the aggressors.

Mr. Young with his profits in mind dispatched Carson and twelve men into the local Indian settlement where they delivered a serious statement. Carson said later in his memoir that they attacked for an

36 Ibid.
37 Ibid.
38 Kenneth L. Holmes, *Ewing Young: Master Trapper* (Portland, Or., The Peter Binford Foundation, 1967), 50.
39 Located in the present city of Frémont, California. Founded on June 11, 1797. It was the fourteenth mission established in California.
40 Randall Milliken, *A Time of Little Choice: The Disintegration of Tribal Culture in the San Francisco Bay Area, 1769–1810* (Menlo Park, Calif.: Ballena Press, 1995), 7–13.

entire day and by sundown the village was burned to the ground.[41] This sort of act was common with early frontiersman before law and order was established years later.

After returning to Yerba Buena and successfully selling off their furs, Young led his men back to the San Gabriel Mission,[42] where they wintered in the nearby Mexican pueblo of Los Angeles. By spring of the following year, Young's party were all safely back in Taos with fat wallets and an itch to get back out into beaver country before another fur company beat them to it. Most importantly, Kit Carson, at the age of twenty-two, was now a bonafide trapper and entering one of the most enjoyable periods of his life.

> We passed time gloriously, spending our money freely, never thinking that our lives had been risked in gaining it. Our only idea was to…have as much pleasure and enjoyment as the country could afford. Trappers and sailors are similar in regard to money that they earn so dearly, being daily in danger of losing their lives. But when the voyage has been made and they have recieved their pay, they think not of the hardships and dangers through which they have passed, but spend all they have and are then ready for another trip.[43]

Pueblo de Los Angeles

Unlike most American cities which were originally built up around the settlement of pioneers, Los Angeles was built by strict orders of the Spanish Governor Felipe de Neve in 1781. The original pueblo, or town, was built according royal Spanish regulations. All farming, from the planting to the sowing, to the size of the fields were fixed by royal decree. Spanish *pobladors* (settlers) were dependents of the Spanish crown and the land they cultivated was not their own.[44] If the poblador failed to till the land he was responsible for, it was taken from him and he was deported from the pueblo.[45] He could

---

41 Carter, *Dear Old Kit*, 47.

42 Utley, *A Life Wild and Perilous*, 112.

43 Carson, *Kit Carson's Autobiography*, 21–22.

44 In 1785, José Francisco Sinova, a laborer, who for a number of years had lived in California, applied for admission into the pueblo and was admitted on the same terms as the original pobladores. See Guinn, *Historical and Biographical Record*, 60.

45 Guinn, *Historical and Biographical Record*, 61.

Kochel & Dresel, Pueblo de Los Angeles, 1857.
Lithograph, Library of Congress.

not buy the land and he could not leave it without permission. On the 4th of September, 1781, the pobladors along with a military escort headed by Governor Felipe de Neve, marched from the Mission San Gabriel to the site selected for their pueblo on the Rio de Porciuncula (now called Los Angeles River). There, with religious ceremonies, the Pueblo de Nuestra Senora La Reina de Los Angeles was formally founded. A mass was said by a priest from the Mission San Gabriel followed by fires of musketry and a procession led by a cross and candlesticks.

The original settlers of Los Angeles were a modest group of forty-four people who had been dispatched from Spanish settlements in Mexico. They were children, young adults and elders of Spanish, Indian and African descent. The population grew very slowly at first, between 1786 and 1790 there were only twenty-one new families who joined the pueblo making its total population 141 souls. By the time Carson passed through in the 1830s, the pueblo was under the Mexican Republic but still had less than 1,000 citizens.

The original site selected for the pueblo was picturesque and romantic. From where Alameda street now is to the eastern bank of the river the land was a dense growth of willows, cottonwoods and alders; while here and there, towered giant sycamores. Wild grape vines and roses also grew throughout this heavenly place.[46]

Summer 1831:

46 Guinn, *Historical and Biographical Record*, 56–60.

Carson's First Trip into the Rocky Mountains

On the fourth of July, 1831, one of the partners in the Rocky Mountain Fur Company, Tom Fitzpatrick, arrived in Santa Fe to obtain supplies for the annual rendezvous happening that year.[47] In addition to supplies, Fitzpatrick also needed more trappers to accompany him through the 500 miles of wilderness that lay between Santa Fe and the rendezvous. He found just the kind of man for the job in brother Carson, who was waiting for such an opportunity. So, once again, Carson set off with a brigade into the Rocky Mountains. The group would travel north until they reached the Platte River and then west following the well-worn trapper trail[48] until they reached the rendezvous site.

Carson ended up living in the Rockies for a full two years before briefly returning to his home in Taos and then again returning to the mountains. Fortunately for Carson, the Rocky Mountain fur trade was just reaching its peak at this time. In his first year in the Rockies, Carson would participate in one of the biggest and most picturesque trapper rendezvous ever in the Wild West.

On a beautiful prairie called "Pierre's Hole" just west of the Grand Teton mountains, mountain men and Indians met up with the three bigs of the industry: Hudson's Bay Company, the American Fur Company (owned by brother John Jacob Astor) and the Rocky Mountain Fur Company.

The 1832 Rendevous

The general course of the trade itself, is laborious and dangerous, full of exposure and privations, and leading to premature exhaustion and disability. Few of those engaged in it reach an advanced stage of life, and still fewer preserve an unbroken constitution. The labor is excessive, subsistence scanty and precarious; and the Indians are ever liable to sudden and violent paroxysms of passions, in which they spare neither friend

47 Willow Valley, about seventy-five miles due north of Salt Lake City, Utah. See Gowans, *Rocky Mountain Rendezvous*, 61

48 This same path would soon become the Oregon Trail.

nor foe.—Brother Lewis Cass[49] writing to brother Andrew Jackson[50] (February 8, 1832)[51]

The weather was unseasonably cold during the summer of 1832, with snow, sleet and hail pushing well into July.[52] The mountain men filed in to Pierre's Hole from the surrounding wilderness, eager to cash in their furs and catch up with their fellows. During this particular year, there were multiple fur companies competing for their business at the rendezvous. For just the cost of transporting supplies like coffee, whiskey, black powder and traps from St. Louis, fur companies could obtain their product directly from the source with no middle man. As a result of this, 1832 was the first year that all of the big fur companies sent supply shipments to the rendezvous.[53]

Once at the designated location, each fur company set up its own separate camp and tried to earn the business of the mountain men. The competition for furs was so fierce, that at the 1833 rendezvous, the American Fur Company (still owned by Brother John Jacob Astor and managed

49 Bro. Cass was initiated as an Entered Apprentice in what is now American Union Lodge Nº 1 at Marietta on December 5, 1803. He achieved his Fellow Craft degree on April 2, 1804, and his Master Mason degree on May 7, 1804. On June 24, 1805, he was admitted as charter member of Lodge of Amity Nº 105 (now Nº 5), Zanesville. He served as the first Worshipful Master of Lodge of Amity in 1806. Cass was one of the founders of the Grand Lodge of Ohio, representing Lodge of Amity at the first meeting on January 4, 1808. He was elected Deputy Grand Master on January 5, 1809, and Grand Master on January 3, 1810, January 8, 1811, and January 8, 1812. See. Thomas J. Melish, *Masonic Journal of Louisville, Ky.: A Monthly Magazine for the Craft* (Wrightson & Co., 1879), 459.

50 His initial lodge membership is unknown, but some evidence suggests that he was a member of Harmony Lodge Nº 1 in 1805. That lodge dissolved in 1808. He served as Grand Master of the Grand Lodge of Tennesee in 1822 and 1823. See Charles Albert Snodgrass, *The History of Freemasonry in Tennessee, 1789-1943* (Nashville, Tenn.: Ambrose Printing Co., 1944), 25.

51 Letter from Lewis Cass to Andrew Jackson, Feb. 8, 1832, "Message from the President of the United States, in Compliance With a Resolution of the Senate Concerning the Fur Trade, and Inland Trade to Mexico, Feb 9, 1832." In Terry Russell, Ed., *Messages from the President on the State of the Fur Trade, 1832–1832* (Fairfield, Wa.: Ye Galleon Press, 1985), 39.

52 Gowans, *Rocky Mountain Rendezvous*, 65.

53 Since 1830, fur companies had been using wagons to transport everything they needed to the rendezvous. These were the first wagon trains to cut tracks in what would become the Oregon Trail in the 1840s. See William E. Hill, *The Oregon Trail: Yesterday and Today* (Caldwell, Idaho: The Caxton Printers, 1992) , 11.

out of St. Louis by Brother Pierre Chouteau[54]) paid $12 per fur to blow all competing companies out of the water.[55] Within a year, one of the smaller companies, the St. Louis Fur Company would fold and within two years the Rocky Mountain Fur Company was out of business.[56]

The buzz in the air from so many different groups of people coming together must have been amazing. It was documented that no less than 400 trappers and 1,000 Indians[57] had assembled at this great rendezvous in addition to their 2,000 to 3,000 horses and mules.[58] Another witness observed there were "about 120 lodges of the Nez Perces and 80 of the Flathead" Indians.[59] All had come together to benefit in this annual trad-

54 Grandson of Pierre Liguest Laclede, the father of St. Louis. Pierre Chouteau was a member of St. Louis Lodge № 111

55 This was an astronomically high price designed to absorb all of the business at the rendezvous. The American Fur Company was ruthless in monopolizing trade.

56 Gowans, *Rocky Mountain Rendezvous*, 98.

57 Frederick G. Young, *The Correspondence and Journals of Captain Nathaniel J. Wyeth, 1831–1836* (New York: Arno Press, 1973), 109.

58 Frances Fuller Victor, *The River of the West: The Adventures of Joe Meek* (Hartford: Conn.: Columbian Book Company, 1870), 101.

59 One of the larger tribes of the Pacific Northwest with an estimated population of between 4,000 and 6,000 members at the time Lewis and Clark met with them on their expedition. See Alvin M. Josephy, *The Nez Perce Indians and the Opening of the Northwest* (Lincoln, Neb.: University of Nebraska Press, 1965), 14.

Alfred Jacob Miller (1810-1874). *Breakfast at Sunrise. 1858.*
Watercolor on paper, The Walters Art Museum, Baltimore, Maryland.

ing event.[60]

The success of this huge rendezvous caused beaver pelts to flood the St. Louis market the following fall. All told, a total of 13,719 pounds of beaver pelts were sold at an average of $4.25 per pound.[61] This equated to $58,305 for the fur companies, roughly $1.3 million in 2016 dollars.[62] Sadly for the beaver population, this meant close to 10,000 less animals in the Rocky Mountains. As horrifying as this may seem, it paled in comparison to what the Hudson's Bay Company was doing on northern bank of the Columbia River. Fort Vancouver was by the early 1830s the most successful, well-organized, and fully self-sufficient fur trading post west of the Rockies.

60 Young, *The Correspondence and Journals*, 159.

61 Gowans, *Rocky Mountain Rendezvous*, 78.

62 *http://www.westegg.com/inflation/infl.cgi.*

The Hudson Bay Company:
Creating a "fur desert" west of the Rockies

With the continued expansion of the fur companies operating in the Rockies, officials with the Hudson's Bay Company knew it was only a matter of time before they started seeing American mountain men trapping in "their" territory. Since its merger with the NWC in 1821, HBC had essentially been the only fur company with the means of maintaining permanent occupation of any lands west of the Rockies and north of Monterey, California. This was owed to the fact that Fort Vancouver sat on some of the richest farm land available and was situated on the fur pipeline that was the Columbia River. Another way to think of Fort Vancouver is that it became everything that Fort Astoria had hoped to become twenty years before.

Capitalizing on this rich farmland was not immediate but rather developed over a few years as a result of economic concerns. Just as the mountain men had to be supplied annually by brigades out of St. Louis, so too were the employees of Fort Vancouver supplied by annual brigades from Hudson's Bay, Manitoba as well as regular ships sent from London.[63] Not only were these shipments extremely expensive but they were inconsistent due to the tricky Columbia River bar which could stall ships for over a month waiting for proper conditions to enter the river.

As a result of the region's extreme isolation, a huge priority was placed on making Fort Vancouver entirely self-sufficient. Governor George Simpson of HBC put much consideration into selecting a site that had excellent soil and access to deep water. The location needed to be able to permanently support hundreds of people and thousands of livestock for decades. Clearly Simpson was successful in his selection as Fort Vancouver became the most important man made structure ever erected in the Pacific Northwest.

It had been two full decades since John Jacob Astor's failed attempt to claim the Columbia River. Everything Astor had hoped for was being materialized by the Hudson's Bay Company—and, to make matters worse, HBC was trying to spread its roots into what it believed would eventually become British soil.[64] Thanks to the Joint Occupation Treaty

---

63 Burt Brown Barker & John McLoughlin, *Letters of Dr. John McLoughlin: Written at Fort Vancouver 1829-1832* (Portland: Oregon Historical Society, 1948), 9.

64 James R. Gibson, *Farming the Frontier: The Agricultural Opening of the Oregon Country, 1786-1846* (Seattle: University of Washington Press, 1985), 27.

of 1818, American and British citizens were allowed to occupy the land. In general however, the only Americans coming to the region were trappers until the first missionaries of 1834. In regards to the former, Hudson's Bay Company was working hard to eliminate the main thing they would be attracted to in the area.

To keep American trappers at bay, the Hudson Bay Company did two things. The first is that McLoughlin established Oregon City in 1829 at Willamette Falls and the second was Simpson's policy to trap as many beaver south of the Columbia River as possible. The idea behind Oregon City was to encourage Americans to settle south of the Columbia River rather than near Fort Vancouver on the north side.[65]

To keep American trappers as far away as possible, the Hudson Bay Company established a policy to purposefully trap as much beaver south of the Columbia River as possible, effectively creating a "fur desert." This fur desert, Simpson thought, would cause American trappers to be less inclined to come to the region economically. By 1831, HBC had essentially "trapped clean" the Snake River country[66] in an attempt to create a buffer zone with the American trappers.[67] Within just a few short years, the Hudson's Bay Company collected over 85,000 beaver pelts from this region alone and brought in $600,000 worth of furs.[68] This estimate was actually quite low compared to the actual number of pelts that HBC clerks took down in their books at Fort Vancouver: 98,288 in 1834, 79,908 in 1835, 46,063 in 1836, and 82,920 in 1837.[69]

It is important to remember that while Americans were hitting the

---

65 Frederick Van Voorhies Holman, *Dr. John McLoughlin: The Father of Oregon* (Cleveland: The A.H. Clark Company, 1907), 42.

66 Southeastern Washington, eastern Oregon, southern Idaho and into western Wyoming.

67 Gibson, *Farming the Frontier*, 15.

68 "In the winters of 1824 and 1825, Mr. Jedediah S. Smith, with a small party of Americans, visited one of the British establishments at the mouth of Flathead river, a branch of the Columbia. Mr. Ogden, who had charge of that post, informed Mr. Smith, rather exultantly, that his party, composed of about sixty men, had taken during their operations in the district of country claimed by the Snake Indians, (a small portion of our territory west of the Rocky mountains) 85 ,000 beaver, equal to ^"150,000, worth say $600,000. The time employed in collecting those furs, as well as I now recollect, was between two and three years." Letter from William H. Ashley to Thomas H. Benton (November, 1827). In James Henry Brown (Ed.), *Brown's Political History of Oregon* (Portland, Or.: Wiley B. Allen, 1892), 1:45–46.

69 Brown, *Brown's Political History of Oregon*, 1:47.

Gustav Sohon. *Fort Vancouver.*
Lithograph, 1854. Oregon Historical Society.

Rocky Mountains hard out of St. Louis and Taos, the British were doing everything they could to eliminate all beavers between the Columbia River and the Rockies. This was not a good time to be a beaver in North America.

From Furs to Farming: The 1830s

When Fort Vancouver first opened, its main objective was to obtain furs and ship them back to York Factory or to London. The fort's secondary objective was to become was to become self-sufficient and not rely on distant aid.[70] Soon, this secondary objective would eclipse the first as the demand for furs started dropping in the mid 1830s and the farms at the fort really started to produce. Fortunately for Hudson's Bay Company, the timing was perfect as starving American emigrants would soon be arriving after crossing the Oregon Trail.

What set Fort Vancouver apart from all other trading posts in the Northwest is that its farms were able to provide more food than was immediately needed by its inhabitants.[71] This created a huge advantage for the Hudson's Bay Company over virtually every other group in the region. In *Guns, Germs, and Steel*, author Jared Diamond highlights that when farming is combined with livestock production, people have longer

70 Gibson, James R. Farming the Frontier. The Agricultural Opening of the Oregon Country, 1786-1846. University of Washington, 1985. 23

71 By the end of 1830, Fort Vancouver had a two year supply of wheat and flour. Gibson, James R. Farming the Frontier. The Agricultural Opening of the Oregon Country, 1786-1846. University of Washington, 1985. 41

Germs that mutate in the pens of livestock are some of the most lethal to the human race. Smallpox, for example, is a mutated version of cowpox. Societies that have lived around domesticated cows gradually become more resistant to smallpox and less prone to outbreaks. Native Americans, on the other hand, had zero contact with cattle prior to European expansion in North America. When someone infected with smallpox came into contact with even one Native American, the effect was like throwing a torch into a thicket of dry brush. Mortality rates in certain tribes was as high as ninety percent of the population. Any contact with smallpox for Indians—whether intentional or accidental—was devastating.[1]

1   Arthur C. Aufderheide, Conrado Rodríguez-Martín, & Odin Langs-joen, *The Cambridge Encyclopedia of Human Paleopathology*. (Cambridge: Cambridge University Press, 1998), 205.

life expectancies, permanent homes, adequate food and milk, fertilizer, transportation, leather, wool and powerful germs.[72]

No one in the Northwest was able to farm more successfully in the first half of the nineteenth century than Hudson's Bay Company. By 1828, Fort Vancouver had over 200 cattle grazing, by 1836 there were 700 and in 1841 there were 3,000.[73] Under very effective management, the fort became Hudson Bay Company's grand emporium and rendezvous west of the Rockies.[74]

Epidemics and Steamboats: 1831

Before steam ships were the norm on the Missouri River, all upriver transportation was done either by man or wind power. Though tedious, man powered paddling, poling or dragging by rope was still more efficient than moving bulky goods on land. When the 1830s came around,

72 Jared Diamond, *Guns, Germs, and Steel: The Fates of Human Societies* (New York: W.W. Norton & Company, 1999), 158.

73 Winther, *The Old Oregon Country*, 71.

74 Gibson, James R. Farming the Frontier. The Agricultural Opening of the Oregon Country, 1786-1846. University of Washington, 1985. 18

Karl Bodmer. *Yellowstone on the Missouri.*
Oil on Canvas, 1832. Joslyn Art Museum, Omaha, Nebraska.

Astor's American Fur Company was so powerful that it upgraded to a steam powered cargo ship to carry furs back to St. Louis.

Over one thousand miles up the Missouri River[75] was an American Fur Company post called Fort Union. In charge of this fort was a true big shot in the industry, the "King of the Missouri,"[76] Kenneth Mackenzie. Mackenzie was in charge of the Rocky Mountain district of the American Fur Company and reported directly to brother Pierre Chouteu in St. Louis.

Mackenzie made two crucial contributions while in charge of Fort Union. One was when he arranged a historic peace treaty with the Blackfoot tribe, effectively securing the entire upper Missouri River fur trade for the AFC.[77] The second was that he urged brother Pierre Chouteu to purchase a

75 Near the modern day border of Montana and North Dakota
76 Dolin, *Fur, Fortune, and Empire,* 271.
77 Dolin, *Fur, Fortune, and Empire,* 272.

steam ship in order to to expedite goods up and down the Missouri river.

Brother Pierre approved, and so in early 1831 a builder out of Louisville, Kentucky was hired to build the first steam ship used in the fur trade. Devouring $10,000 of the American Fur Company's capital, the 130-foot long *Yellowstone* would revolutionize how trade was conducted on the Missouri River and further secure the American Fur Company's monopoly over the region.[78]

In June of 1832, the *Yellowstone* made its way through all of the snags and hazards of the river to reach Fort Union.[79] Once loaded down with furs, it turned around and covered an incredible 100 miles per day in its return.[80] This was a significant development for the American Fur Company's income and efficiency.

For the Indian population of the upper Missouri River, steamboats would bring one of the worst epidemics they had ever seen. In the summer of 1837, the American Fur Company had not one but two steam ships traveling up and down the river. One of their ships, *St. Peter's*, was on its way to Fort Union to deliver supplies in addition to several passengers infected with smallpox. It was well known by this point that Indians had no defense against the disease. Even though efforts were taken to prevent contact with the infected passengers, the Indians were accustomed to boarding the ships when they pulled up to a post. When the ship stopped at Fort Mandan and Fort Union, Indians rejected warnings and boarded anyway, infecting themselves and starting an epidemic. All told, over 17,000 Indians died of smallpox within a few months from the Mandan, Minataree, Arikara, Sioux, Assiniboin and Blackfoot tribes[81]. It was a horrific outbreak that left countless bodies "unburied…while the few survivors fled," further spreading the disease.[82]

The Buffalo Robe Trade: The 1830s to the 1860s

In addition to the thousands of beaver pelts being brought back to St.

---

78   Hiram Martin Chittenden, *The American Fur Trade of the Far West* (New York: F.P. Harper, 1902), 340.

79   Dolin, *Fur, Fortune, and Empire*, 274.

80   Dolin, *Fur, Fortune, and Empire*, 274.

81   Chittenden, *The American Fur Trade*, 620-27.

82   W. P. Clark, *The Indian Sign Language* (Philadelphia: L. R. Hamersly & Co, 1885), 351–52.

Louis on steam ships, there was a new fur in demand during this time. The largest and most quintessential animal of the Wild West was now the most desired fur by American consumers.[83] The mighty buffalo (or bison as they are now called) would be hunted down to near extinction as a result.

With the beaver trade waning, the buffalo robe trade was about to blow open. From 1815 to 1830, an average of 26,000 buffalo robes were sold annually at market in St. Louis.[84] From 1830–1860, that number skyrocketed to an annual average of 100,000 robes.[85] Eventually, the population was hunted down from an (estimated) original population of over 30 million to just over 1,000 animals in 1889.[86] This sickening thought is only remedied by the fact that today thanks to conservation efforts, the American bison has recovered to over 500,000 animals in North America.[87]

The End of an Era

The fur trade had to come to an end eventually, either through diminishing supply or shrinking demand. There were many reasons why the fur trade slowed down in the 1830s, most apparent was the widespread depletion of the beaver population.

With the writing on the wall, brother Astor diversified his portfolio as his profits began to decline. What had started out as a simple apprenticeship under a New York fur trader[88] had grown into a complete monopolization

83 Dolin, *Fur, Fortune, and Empire,* 302.

84 Chittenden, *The American Fur Trade,* 7.

85 John E. Sunder, *The Fur Trade on the Upper Missouri, 1840–1865* (Norman, Okla.: University of Oklahoma Press, 1993), 17.

86 Andrew C. Isenberg, *The Destruction of the Bison: An Environmental History, 1750–1920* (Cambridge, Mass.: Cambridge University Press, 2000), 24–30; William Temple Hornaday, *The Extermination of the American Bison* (Washington, D.C.: Smithsonian Institution Press, 2002), 180.

87 Curtis H. Freese, K. Aune, D. Boyd, James N. Derr, Steven C. Forrest, C. Cormack Gates, Peter J. Gogan, Shaun M. Grassel, Natalie D. Halbert, Kyran Kunkel, & K. Redford, "Second Chance for the Plains Bison." *Biological Conservation* 136 (2007): 175–84.

88 After hearing about the fur trade on his way over to America, young Astor was urged by his older brother to seek out an experienced fur trader in New York City. As a result, John Jacob Astor met Robert Bowne, an "aged and benevolent Quaker" who had long been in the business of buying and exporting furs. Astor lived as an apprentice in Mr. Bowne's house and made $2 a week. Through this apprenticeship, Astor learned the trade and developed an eye for fine furs. He soon was dispatched

Brother Oscar Wilde in a fur coat. 1882, New York.
Photo by Napoleon Sarony (1821-1896).

of the entire North American fur trade. He was by the early 1830s one of the richest men in the world and certainly the richest man in America. According to one study, Astor is the fifth richest American of all time, leaving behind a net worth of over $121 billion dollars when adjusted for inflation.[89] Not to mention, his rags to riches story is truly one of the greatest examples of the American dream. Astor's American Fur Company held a complete monopoly on not only the Missouri River but also the Mississippi River and Great Lakes region.[90] This territory covered the entire upper half of the United States.

out as far as Montreal to purchase furs and live the life of a fur trader. By 1790, just seven years after he arrived in America, he opened his own business at 40 Little Dock Street (now Water Street near the Brooklyn Bridge). See James Parton, *Life of John Jacob Astor* (New York: The American News Company, 1865), 33–40.

89 1. John D. Rockefeller, 2. Andrew Carnegie 3. Corneilius Vanderbilt 4. Bill Gates. See *http://www.businessinsider.com/richest-americans-ever-2011-4#5-john-jacob-astor-9*, accessed August 10, 2016.

90 Dolin, *Fur, Fortune, and Empire*, 275.

When the price for beaver furs plummeted by over 30% in 1933,[91] Astor sold his 51% of the AFC and "retired" from the business, only to become wildly successful in New York City real estate. Though the "Napoleon of Commerce" was leaving the fur trade, mountain men still had a few good years before they too would have to hang up their traps and find other work.[92]

The Last Good Year of the Rendezvous: 1833

The rendezvous of 1833 was said to be the last "good year, for with 1834 came the spoilers—the idlers, the missionaries, the hard seekers after the money."[93] Approximately 165 packs of beaver at 100 pounds per pack left the Green River rendezvous that year bound for St. Louis. The packs were unloaded and sold for a total of $60,000[94] which was then paid out across the four fur companies who had brought the furs back.

During the winter of 1833-1834, as mentioned earlier, Astor sold his shares in the AFC which changed the leadership in the company. Brother Pierre Chouteu along with Bernard Pratte bought Astor's shares and became de facto heads of its Western department.[95] Along with this shift in leadership came an interesting new chapter for the Wild West. In 1834, the first pair of American missionaries crossed the Rockies in an attempt to Christianize the peoples of the Pacific Northwest.

The missionaries were Daniel and Jason Lee and they had come on behalf of the Methodist Church. Just what were men of the cloth doing around a bunch of mountain men "scoundrels"?[96] They had not come to preach against their sinful ways. What they were actually doing was accompanying the trappers in order to meet with Indians of the Pacific Northwest.[97]

The story of how the Methodist Church came up with the idea of

91 Dolin, *Fur, Fortune, and Empire*, 281.

92 "For nearly 40 years, Astor has been characterized as, perhaps, the greatest merchant of this, if not any age-the Napoleon of commerce." See "John Jacob Astor," *The Merchants Magazine and Commercial Review* (July to December, 1844), 154.

93 Don Berry, *A Majority of Scoundrels: An Informal History of the Rocky Mountain Fur Company* (New York: Harper, 1961), 336.

94 Gowans, *Rocky Mountain Rendezvous*, 96.

95 Gowans, *Rocky Mountain Rendezvous*, 103.

96 Gowans, *Rocky Mountain Rendezvous*, 94.

97 *The Quarterly of the Oregon Historical Society* (1919), 163.

heading into the Wild West to deliver the gospel has to be one of the most remarkable stories about faith and missionary work. Its origins go back to the Lewis and Clark expedition of 1806 when Clark met with the Nez Perce Indians on his way back to Missouri. At this time, Clark no doubt talked with many tribal members and left a deep impression on them. So deep, apparently, that in 1831, over twenty-five years later, four Salish Indians showed up in St. Louis to meet with Brother William Clark.[98] To get to St. Louis, they walked over 2,000 miles across the continent with hope of finding religion.[99] News about this remarkable event took a few years to spread but, in 1833, a story was published by the *Christian Advocate* in New York. The article sensationalized how these Indians had come in search of the white man's "Book of Heaven."[100]

Whether or not the four Indians were in fact looking for the Bible has been debated ever since, but what happened as a result of their visit changed the course of American history.

The story in the *Christian Advocate* caused a major stir among evangelicals, effectively creating a call to arms. As a result, in 1834 the Church dispatched Reverend Jason Lee and his nephew Daniel Lee to head west to establish a mission in Indian country.[101]

The two brave missionaries accompanied a brigade of more than thirty trappers heading to the rendezvous that year out of Independence, Missouri.[102] After attending the rendezvous and seeing the "whooping, hollering and quarrelling,"[103] they continued on all the way to Fort Vancouver.[104] At the fort, they were warmly received by Dr. John McLoughlin who listened to the men explain the reason for their arrival. McLoughlin responded that it was:

> Too dangerous for them to establish a mission (in Flathead country); to do good to the Indians, they must establish themselves where

---

98 Indigenous peoples of the Pacific Northwest Coast.

99 Harry R. Ritter, *Washington's History: The People, Land, and Events of the Far Northwest* (Portland: WestWinds Press, 2003), 48.

100 Thomas Crosby, *Among the An-ko-me-nums or Flathead Tribes of Indians of the Pacific Coast* (W. Briggs, 1907), 14.

101 Ritter, *Washington's History*, 48.

102 Gowans, *Rocky Mountain Rendezvous*, 104.

103 Gowans, *Rocky Mountain Rendezvous*, 98.

104 Crosby, *Among the An-ko-me-nums*, 16.

they could…teach them first to cultivate the ground and live more comfortably than they do by hunting, and as they do this, teach them religion; that the Willamette afforded them a fine field, and that they ought to go there, and they would get the same assistance as the settlers. They followed my advice and went to the Willamette.[105]

Reverend Lee selected a site for his mission in Willamette Valley about ten miles north of modern day Salem, Oregon.[106] This little nucleus would grow as more missionaries were sent as reinforcements.

In addition to his advice, McLoughlin also lent livestock from Fort Vancouver to the desperate missionaries. In what would become his custom of helping many American emigrants to come, McLoughlin lent the mission several cows, a bull and oxen to establish their settlement.[107] McLoughlin, a God-fearing man himself, even donated $130 of his own money to aid in the mission's efforts. The gift included this letter:

Dear Sir:

I do myself the pleasure to hand you the enclosed subscription, which the gentlemen who have signed it request you will do them the favor to accept for the use of the Mission: and they pray our Heavenly Father, without whose assistance we can do nothing, that of his infinite mercy he will vouchsafe to bless and prosper your pious endeavors, and believe me to be, with esteem and regard, your sincere well-wisher and humble servant.

John McLoughlin[108]

It is understandable that McLoughlin was so generous at this time, as these missionaries were not patriots looking to claim the land nor were they trappers looking to compete for furs. With the roots of the first American Mission now planted on the Pacific Coast, let us turn back to the Rocky Mountains where a star was rising among the mountain men.

---

105 Holman, *Dr. John McLoughlin*, 55.
106 Holman, *Dr. John McLoughlin*, 56.
107 Holman, *Dr. John McLoughlin*, 57.
108 Gustavus Hines, *Oregon: Its History, Condition, and Prospects* (Buffalo, N.Y., 1851), 16.

Alfred Jacob Miller (1810–1874). *Greeting the Trappers.*
Watercolor on paper, 1850. Buffalo Bill Center of the West, Cody, Wyoming.

Kit Carson's Famous Duel at the Rendezvous: 1835

The rendezvous of 1835 included not only a duel between two mountain men, but also a surgery performed by an actual doctor. The latter was performed by Dr. Marcus Whitman, who like Jason Lee the year before was at the rendezvous because he was on his way to Oregon Country to investigate starting a mission. The notes he took while at the rendezvous provide us with a striking visual:

> Most of the trappers and traders of the mountains are here and about two thousand Shoshoni Indians and about forty lodges of Nez Perce Indians.[109]

Further,

> I extracted an arrow point from the back of James Bridger, one of the partners of the company which had been shot by the Blackfeet Indians

109 Archer B. Hulbert, *Overland to the Pacific* (Denver: Denver Public Library, 1932-1941), Vol 2:34.

near three years previous; and one from another man which had been shot in by the same Indians about a year before. These Indians and trappers often fight and both seem mutually to exult in each others destruction.[110]

While at the rendezvous, Dr. Whitman met with members of the Nez Perce tribe and discussed possibly building a mission on their land which they obliged him in doing. As a result, Whitman returned to the States and recruited more missionaries to help him establish a settlement near Fort Nez Perce[111]. While Whitman arranged plans with the Indians, a different kind of meeting was taking place. This one involved a whiskey fueled "bully of the mountains"[112] who was causing trouble with our very own Bro. Kit Carson.

> A hunter (named Joseph Chouinard[113])…mounted his horse with a loaded rifle, and challenged any Frenchman, American, Spaniard or Dutchman, to fight him in single combat. Kit Carson told him that if he wished to die, he would accept the challenge. Carson mounted his horse, and with a loaded pistol, rushed into close contact, and both almost at the same instant fired. Carson's ball entered Chouinard's hand, came out at the wrist and passed through the arm above the elbow. Chouinard's ball passed over the head of Carson; and while he went for another pistol, Shunar begged that his life might be spared.[114]

Carson was only twenty-five years old at the time but the duel started the legend that would follow him for the rest of his days. After the rendezvous broke up, Carson would join a brigade led by Jim Bridger who had just had the arrowhead removed from his back.

---

110 LeRoy Reuben Hafen, *Mountain Men and the Fur Trade of the Far West: Eighteen Biographical Sketches* (Glendale, Calif.: Arthur H. Clark Company, 1965–1972), 152.

111 Founded in 1818 by the North West Company and after 1821 it was run by Hudson's Bay Company until its closure in 1857. See William H. Gray, *A History of Oregon, 1792–1849, Drawn from Personal Observation and Authentic Information* (Portland, Or.: Harris & Holman, 1870), 143–44.

112 Gowans, *Rocky Mountain Rendezvous*, 123.

113 Sides, "Blood and Thunder," 38.

114 Samuel Parker, *Journal of an Exploring Tour Beyond the Rocky Mountains* (Auburn, N.Y.: J.C. Derby & Company, 1846), 83.

John C. Frémont. c. 1856
Lithograph by Crehan after Saintin. Library of Congress

Carson said later in his memoirs that "these were the happiest days of my life."[115] The freedom of living moment to moment, day-to-day in the wilderness must have been exhilarating. However, the trade only had a few good years left as the supply of their product was being wiped out. Carson later recalled that "beaver was getting scarce, it became necessary to try our hand at something else."[116]

Carson went where there was work and eventually that took him to Fort Bent,[117] where he hunted for game, earning a dollar a day to make

115 H.R. Tilton & Usher L. Burdick, *The Last Days of Kit Carson* (Grand Forks, N.D.: Holt Printing Company, 1939), 5.

116 Carter, *Dear Old Kit*, 77.

117 A major buffalo robe trading fort on the Santa Fe trail located in southeastern Colorado.

Carol M. Highsmith. *Independence Rock.*
c. 2016. Library of Congress.

ends meet.[118] In 1842, he decided it was time for him and his two daughters to return to Missouri to reconnect with his family. This would be the first time in sixteen years he had been back to the United States. He put his daughters into the care of his family members in Missouri and got on a steamer heading back up the Missouri River. On this boat Carson met a man who would sweep him into his biggest adventure yet.[119]

Carson Hired as Guide for the Frémont Expeditions: Summer of 1842

There are times in a man's life where his fate seems to be decided by chance encounters. For Carson, the day he met John Frémont was one such day as it completely altered his life's path. Carson was only thirty-two years old, Frémont being his junior by four years, but the connection between the two was nearly immediate.

Having just spent the previous decade of his life on trapping expeditions all over the west coast, Carson was the perfect guide for Frémont as he mapped the West. Carson joined twenty-one other men in Frémont's

118 Hafen, *Mountain Men and the Fur Trade*, 175.
119 Hafen, *Mountain Men and the Fur Trade*, 176.

Other impressive feats on Frémont's first expedition:

    1. Discovered a beautiful lake at the western foot of the Wind River Mountains (now called Lake Frémont).

    2. Climbed a 13,000 foot mountain (now called Frémont Peak) in the Wind River Range without the aid of ropes, cramp-ons or any mountaineering experience.

    3. Frémont and a few voyageurs went white water rafting in a primitive rubber boat in order to survey the upper part of the Platte River. Unexpectedly they hit bad rapids, flipped, lost all their books, journals, scientific instruments and nearly drowned. Downriver they recovered their gear and climbed out of the steep canyon to rejoin the rest of the group.

first expedition, mostly Creole and Canadian voyageurs out of St. Louis.[120] Additionally, a twelve-year-old boy joined in for the adventure of a lifetime. He was the son of Missouri Senator and Freemason Thomas Hart Benton.[121] Carson would bring first hand experience to the team as they mapped the Platte River.[122]

The first notable event in their journey happened on the 28th of June when they crossed paths with a party of fourteen American Fur Company trappers on their way back from Fort Laramie.[123] The men were marching along the banks of the river carrying huge packs of furs on their backs. It turned out they had left the fort originally on a boat but had to abandon it due to the low and unpredictable waters of the Platte River. With no other transportation, they chose to carry the valuable packs on their backs for hundreds of miles. Imagine carrying a huge block on your back that weighs anywhere from 60 to 100 pounds for one day. Now repeat that every

---

120 Frémont, *Oregon and California*, 6.

121 A charter member of Missouri Lodge N° 12. See Ray V. Denslow, *Territorial Masonry: The Story of Freemasonry and the Louisiana Purchase* (Washington, D.C., The Masonic Service Association of the United States, 1925), 56.

122 John Charles Frémont, *Oregon and California: The Exploring Expedition to the Rocky Mountains, Oregon and California. To which is Added a Description of the Physical Geography of California. With Recent Notices of the Gold Region from the Latest and Most Authentic Sources* (Buffalo: George H. Derby & Co., 1851), 107.

123 Frémont, *Oregon and California*, 18.

Alfred Jacob Miller (1810–1874). *The Devils Gate*.
Oil on canvas, The Walters Museum, Baltimore.

Alfred Jacob Miller was the first artist to sketch Devil's Gate, a vertical rock formation
and four-hundred-foot canyon cut by the Sweetwater River in Wyoming. Although
travelers through the region did not pass through the canyon, the sighting of Devil's
Gate was a major landmark for those on the Oregon Trail.

day for a month. That's what these trappers were willing to do to get paid.

After a whirlwind tour up and down the Platte River, Frémont returned to St. Louis in the fall of 1842. He took a steamer to the District of Columbia, where he reported on his findings. As a result of this trip, accurate maps were created showing exact distances between landmarks. These maps would become priceless in years to come as they would help open up the Oregon Trail to hundreds of thousands of American emigrants.

Just six months after his first trip, Frémont assembled another team to set out farther into the West.[124] This time, Frémont's expedition would go all the way through Oregon country and into Alta California. In May of 1843, the second Frémont expedition set out from St. Louis to put more parts of the West on the map.

In July, the group reached St. Vrain's Fort[125] in what is now north central Colorado where he had "the satisfaction to meet our good buffalo hunter of 1842, Christopher Carson, whose services I considered myself fortunate to secure again."[126] Frémont also considered Carson his "true and reliable friend."[127]

The diverse group of hunters, voyageurs and surveyors spread out as they combed the countryside. Each day they assembled into one camp where they compared notes and wrote reports about the day. Some days they ate fresh game while other days they had to settle for salted pork which they had as a backup.

In August the group reached the landmark of the "Devil's Gate" and noted a well worn wagon road heading to Oregon.[128] This road would

124 Frémont, *Oregon and California*, 123.

125 A fort built in North Central Colorado owned and operated by Colonel Ceran St. Vrain. St. Vrain was raised a Master Mason on January 25, 1855 at Montezuma Lodge No- 109 in New Mexico). After a visit to Fort Laramie in mid July they they reached Independence Rock in central Wyoming where Frémont noted a curious feature for 1842. He said the rock was already well carved with the names of people who had passed by it before. Interestingly enough, it was upon this rock just twenty years later that a group of Master Masons convened and met for the first masonic meeting in Wyoming. See Walter C. Reusser, *History of the Grand Lodge of Ancient, Free and Accepted Masons of Wyoming 1874–1974*. (Laramie, Wy.: The Grand Lodge of Ancient, Free and Accepted Masons of Wyoming, 1975), 1.

126 Frémont, *Oregon and California*, 141.

127 Frémont, *Oregon and California*, 146

128 Frémont, *Oregon and California*, 161.

Albert Bierstadt. *Lake Tahoe.*
Oil on canvas, 1868. Harvard Art Museums.

become busier with each advancing year and by the half way point of the
century, over ten thousand emigrants would have used it. For the Indians of
the region, the wagon road meant a drastic drop in the buffalo population.
The vast herds that once roamed the plains were now mainly centered
around the eastern foothills of the Rocky Mountains. Starting in the
1840s, several Indian Nations were growing concerned at the lack of their
principal food supply.[129] But contrary to popular mythos, emigrant trains
certainly weren't the main reason for the buffalo's decline. Rather it was
the American Fur Company who were killing over 70,000 buffalo a year
to keep up with the demand for the popular buffalo robes. It is surprising
the iconic animal didn't go extinct by the midpoint of the century at the
rate they were being killed.

129 Frémont, *Oregon and California*, 189.

In the early part of fall, Frémont and his men reached Fort Hall[130] in southern Idaho.[131] Just five years later, this location would be where the first Masonic charter in the West would change hands before making its way to Oregon City. Additionally they were now in the Snake River country, the same desolate landscape that had sorely tested Brother Hunt and his party three decades prior. Frémont described it as "a melancholy and strange looking country—one of fracture and violence and fire."[132] They continued surveying the terrain westward until they reached another HBC post called Fort Boise. This post was noted as a simple dwelling house on the right bank of the Snake River.[133]

After stopping at Whitman's mission, Fort Nez Perce and the Dalles, Frémont finally arrived at Fort Vancouver in November.[134] This was the end of his official mission to connect the maps from his first expedition to those of Lieutenant Charles Wilkies.[135] However, instead of returning to the States as originally planned, Frémont decided to take a detour through Alta California and map the unknown Sierra Mountains. Frémont could not resist the opportunity to study "new geographical, botanical and geological science."[136]

After restocking their rations, hiring new men, and purchasing one hundred horses from Fort Vancouver, they set off into the winter conditions. Some nights the thermometer dipped into the single digits.[137] These were the days of heavy wool and leather rather than today's gore-tex, down and synthetic materials.

130 Built in 1834 by speculators out of Boston. Later sold to Hudson's Bay Company

131 Frémont, *Oregon and California*, 216.

132 Frémont, *Oregon and California*, 224.

133 Frémont, *Oregon and California*, 233. It was near this location in 1854, that the first Master of the Verity Lodge № 59 in 1890 (the author's current lodge), David F. Neely, passed through as a young boy. He was crossing the Oregon Trail with his family and a large wagon party when they were attacked by Shoshone Indians leaving nine dead Americans and twelve dead Indians after the skirmish. It was thereafter known as the Boise Massacre. See Donald H. Shannon, *The Boise Massacre on the Oregon Trail* (2004), 83-89.

134 Frémont, *Oregon and California*, 249 & 256.

135 Frémont was working under Colonel J.J. Abert, Chief of the Corps of Topographical Engineers. See Frémont, *Oregon and California*, 123.

136 Frémont, *Oregon and California*, 271.

137 Frémont, *Oregon and California*, 276.

Modoc National Forest.
Photo by Jim Gumm. Wikimedia Commons.

Frémont clearly had ambitions to have his named etched into history, so he defied logic and pushed his men into the freezing unknown. In December they arrived at Lake Klamath, a massive body of water in southern Oregon. Reports about the area warned of hostile Indians so to make a firm statement about their presence, Frémont ordered a cannon to be fired out across the lake. Within minutes, all of the smoke from campfires around the lake went out and Frémont's group was able to pass through the area unchallenged.[138]

They continued trudging south into Alta California where they battled deep snow in the northern part of the Sierra Nevada Mountains. On the eastern side of this range, Frémont came to a lake which he named after a striking natural feature that reminded him of the pyramids of Egypt (see image on next page).[139]

---

138 Frémont, *Oregon and California*, 283.

139 "From the point that we viewed it, presented a pretty exact outline of the great pyramid of Cheops. This striking feature suggested a name for the lake, and I called it Pyramid Lake." Frémont, *Oregon and California*, 306.

Timothy O'Sullivan (1840–1882). *The Pyramid and Domes, Pyramid Lake.*
c. 1867. Library of Congress.

They were entering a land that had rarely if ever been seen by any Americans except a handful of trappers. Even the Indians they met spoke a language no one had heard before and interactions were strictly through gestures and signs.[140]

It would be untrue to say that the Indians they met were unfriendly to the American explorers. To the contrary, Frémont's party was routinely approached by random Indians who presented them with gifts. One such interaction involved the presentation of a salmon which Frémont affectionately referred to as "superior to that of any fish I have ever known. Extraordinary size, two to four feet long."[141]

Upon reaching one settlement of Indians, Frémont inquired if anyone would be willing to guide his group over the mountains. This would be an incredible feat in the summer let alone in January when the snow would be well over their heads. Because of this, many of the tribal members shook

140 Frémont, *Oregon and California*, 313.
141 Frémont, *Oregon and California*, 307.

George A. Crofutt. *American Progress.*
Chromolithograph after a painting by John Gast, c. 1873. Library of Congress.

their heads at the idea saying it would be impossible.[142]

Despite warnings that they would surely die if they attempted to make a pass in winter conditions, Frémont ordered his group up into the Sierra Nevada Mountains. With visions of the sunny Sacramento valley on the other side, the men followed his orders and kicked a path through the snow.

Eventually they found a pass (later called Carson Pass)[143] through the 9,000 foot mountain range. Upon reaching a summit which allowed them to see far beyond into the west, Brother Kit Carson recognized a mountain from his trapping days.[144] Confident they were at least heading in the right direction, they had to march through towering snow drifts and battle snow blindness with simple black silk handkerchiefs over their eyes.[145]

---

142 Frémont, *Oregon and California*, 326.

143 Hampton Sides, *Blood and Thunder: The Epic Story of Kit Carson and the Conquest of the American West* (New York: Anchor Books, 2007), 75.

144 Frémont, *Oregon and California*, 330.

145 Frémont, *Oregon and California*, 333.

It was late February of 1844 when they finally started to descend the western slope of the Sierra Mountains. "Life yet!" Carson yelled one day upon seeing a hillside covered in fresh grass.[146] One can only imagine the effect that the warm sun and fragrant California poppies had on the men. But before everyone could rejoice, one man had a mental break down and lost his mind. One day he jumped into a frigid and raging river as if he was taking a dip to cool off in the summer time.[147]

With the brutal cold Sierra's behind them, every step they took brought them closer to the warm California climate. Soon they noticed beautiful "evergreen oaks" which Frémont called "live-oaks" to discern them from other species.[148] These trees are a normal sight for Californians today but to Frémont they were remarkable.

In March they came to a large Indian "ranchera" where Frémont noted the residents spoke broken Spanish.[149] Additionally they were informed that they were now only a few days away from Sutter's Fort.[150]

In addition to much needed rest, Frémont obtained 130 new horses and 30 cows from Fort Sutter.[151] They were advised to head southeast from the fort and connect with a Spanish trail that would take them back to Santa Fe. Unlike the California of today, large wildlife such as elk, wild horses, grizzly bears, wolves and antelope were seen in abundance as they followed what is today highway 99 through Fresno and Bakersfield.[152]

Around the southern edge of the Sierra Mountains, Frémont noted that there were no rivers that flowed from the Rockies into San Francisco Bay. Instead, there were only two relatively short rivers, the San Joaquin and Sacramento which came from the Sierras.[153] This conclusion meant that travel and communication on the west coast would have to go north and south rather than east to west. Additionally, the Columbia River was the sole river that connected the Pacific ocean to the Rockies. Thanks to

---

146 Frémont, *Oregon and California*, 343.

147 Frémont, *Oregon and California*, 344.

148 Frémont, *Oregon and California*, 345.

149 Frémont, *Oregon and California*, 351.

150 Built by John Sutter who had arrived in Alta, California in 1839. The fort included blacksmiths, a commons, distillery, twelve canons and was capable of hosting up to one hundred troops. See Frémont, *Oregon and California*, 354.

151 Frémont, *Oregon and California*, 356.

152 Frémont, *Oregon and California*, 361.

153 Frémont, *Oregon and California*, 369.

Albert Bierstadt. *Surveyors Wagon in the Rockies.*
c. 1859. Oil paint on paper. Saint Louis Art Museum, St. Louis, Missouri.

this information, the United States would be able to fully assess the value of particular regions on the Pacific coast.

Frémont Returns to the States via the Old Spanish Trail: 1844

Satisfied with a sweeping tour through the Wild West, Frémont turned back for the United States. The expedition had surveyed thousands of miles of terrain, filled journals with priceless scientific information and most importantly, solidified Frémont's name as an American hero. But before Fremont and his men could return to their normal lives, they would face a series of challenges unlike those in the first half of the journey. The hardened group of men would now travel through a series of deserts full of unique sights. The first was the Mohave desert where Frémont noted the Yucca tree and described it as "the most repulsive tree in the vegetable kingdom."[154]

154 Frémont, *Oregon and California*, 370.

In addition to plant and animal diversities, each geographical region was populated by people with unique customs and appearances. One night they were approached by Mohave Indians who spoke Spanish.[155] Another day they were approached by a pair of Mexicans who came riding up to them on horseback—a man and a boy. The man's name was Adreas Fuentes and the boy, eleven years old, named Pablo Hernandez. They had been separated from a larger group while returning from the Pueblo de Los Angeles.[156] A group of hostile Indians had attacked their group in order to steal their horses. Andreas and Pablo fled for their lives which led them to meeting Frémont's group.

After some questioning about where the event had taken place, Frémont's party changed course and went to investigate. Here Brother Carson and another guide named Godey tracked the direction the Indians had fled with the stolen horses. What happened next was straight out of a classic western movie.

Carson and Godey sped off into the hills with intentions of avenging the innocent lives lost. By dusk, they located the horse thieves' camp and hid nearby until daybreak. At dawn, they surprised the guilty party

155 They had learned Spanish while living at one of the Spanish Missions on the Coast before it had broken up. Frémont, *Oregon and California*, 376.

156 Frémont, *Oregon and California*, 377.

by firing their rifles from long range, injuring two of the Indians while the rest fled for their lives. Carson and Godey rode into the camp and rounded up all the horses. But before they departed, they left a message for the blood thirsty thieves by scalping two Indians who lay injured on the ground.

All told, they rode 100 miles in twenty four hours and returned with the stolen horses. Astounded by the turn of events, Frémont called it the "boldest and most disinterested which the annals of western adventure, so full of daring deeds, can present. Two men, in a savage desert, pursue day and night an unknown body of Indians, into the defile of an unknown mountain—attack them on sight, without counting numbers—and defeat them in an instant—and for what? To punish the robbers…and avenge the wrongs of Mexicans whom they did not known."[157]

The following day they returned to the site where Andreas and Pablo had been attacked. Frémont noted that: "The dead silence of the place was ominous; and, galloping rapidly up, we found only the corpses of the two men: everything else was gone. They were naked, mutilated, and pierced with arrows. One had evidently fought, and with desperation…one of his hands, and both his legs, had been cut off.[158]

After taking in the gruesome scene and realizing the boy's mother had been kidnapped by the thieves, Carson could be assured his attack the previous day was most appropriate. Evidently, the Indians who lived in the surrounding mountains prayed on the caravans as they passed through the valley.

The next landmark they came to was the Las Vegas "camping ground" which was nothing more than a marshy plain.[159] Frémont's caravan was quite conspicuous here, due to the large herd of animals he had brought with him. One evening they were surrounded by a large group of Indians armed with bows and arrows. Frémont assumed they were of the same tribe that had killed Pablo's family.

A man who appeared to be the leader, forced himself into Frémont's camp and boasted that even though Frémont had over twenty men armed with rifles, the Indians were much stronger as he twanged his bow.[160] This

157 Frémont, *Oregon and California*, 381–82.
158 Frémont, *Oregon and California*, 384
159 Frémont, *Oregon and California*, 387
160 Frémont, *Oregon and California*, 388

threat was enough to cause Brother Carson to jump up and threaten him, "Don't say that, old man." After a tense standoff, the Indians left after they were given an old tired horse from Frémont.

The following morning, camp was broken up and the men fanned out to continue surveying the landscape. At one point in the day, one of the French voyageurs in the group wandered off to fetch a stray mule and never returned. Around the time his absence was noted, a plume of smoke was seen in the distance which often signaled a warning among Indians.[161]

Carson and several others galloped off in the direction of the smoke. As it was now dusk, it was difficult to track him but they were able to find a butchered mule and a puddle of blood presumed to be from the missing voyageur.[162] The men returned to the main camp after an exhaustive search of the area. On the following morning a larger search party combed the area where they had found the blood but no trace of man or horse could be found. It was determined that the Indians had killed the voyageur and thrown him into a river.

It was now May and Frémont's men were equally saddened by the loss of one of their best men and enraged that these "Arabs of the New World" had killed their dear friend.[163] After much consideration, they decided to not seek revenge in the unknown mountains. This proved to be a wise decision for after several days travel they crossed paths with the famed trapper, Joseph Walker,[164] who was leading a caravan from California.[165]

Frémont and Walker's men set up camp and decided to join forces in their return to the States. What a blessing it was for Frémont to have met such an experienced guide in the middle of what is now southwest Utah. There were no more run ins with hostile Indians to speak of and the scientific purpose of the journey was able to continue.

Towards the end of May, 1844, they reached the grayish waters of Lake Utah, which meant they had essentially completed their explora-

---

161 Frémont noted on multiple occasions throughout the West that Indians would alert each other of danger by the use of smoke signals. See Frémont, *Oregon and California*, 390.

162 Frémont, Oregon and California, 391

163 Frémont, Oregon and California, 391

164 Joseph Reddeford Walker was perhaps the most famous of all mountain men. By 1844 he had already spent time in the Rockies and attended many rendezvous, had helped survey the Santa Fe Trail, trapped and guided for Benjamin Bonneville

165 Frémont, Oregon and California, 394

146

Joseph Walker.
Photo by Mathew Brady, c. 1860. Wikimedia Commons.

tion of new territory. Frémont and his men had in effect made a giant
loop around the Great Salt Lake since September of the previous year.

"The circuit which we had made…had cost us eight months of time,
and 3,500 miles of traveling, had given us a view of Oregon and of North

California from the Rocky Mountains to the Pacific Ocean."

In addition to valuable information on new plants, animals, mountain passes and other geographical features, Frémont's reports confirmed the "value beyond estimation" of the Columbia River to the United States.[166]

On July 1st they arrived at Bent's Fort where Walker and Carson stayed for the winter. Frémont and the rest of the men (including young Pablo Hernandez and Andreas Fuentes) continued back to Missouri.[167]

It is incredible that in the fourteen months spent in the Wild West, not one case of sickness had occurred among Frémont's group. There were three deaths: one due to a mental breakdown, one from Indians, and one by an accidental gunshot. Nonetheless, the expedition was an overwhelming success and of considerable influence to the destiny of the United States.

On the 6th of August, Frémont reached St. Louis, where the group disbanded. Many of the French men on the expedition returned to their homes in St. Louis. Andreas and Pablo, the two Mexicans who had joined Frémont in the Mojave Desert went on to live interesting lives in the States.[168] Pablo, eleven years old, went to live with Bro. Thomas Hart Benton and received a proper education while Andreas ended up working with Frémont on his third expedition the following year.

Upon returning to D.C., Frémont delivered his reports which were rapidly disseminated into 10,000 copies available to the public.[169] Though he would lead bigger and more consequential expeditions into the West, it was this 1843–1844 expedition that helped accelerate the movement known as Manifest Destiny.[170]

166 Frémont, Oregon and California, 401
167 Frémont, *Oregon and California*, 426.
168 Frémont, *Oregon and California*, 426.
169 Bil Gilbert, *The Old West: The Trailblazers* (New York: Time-Life Books, 1973), 163.
170 Frémont, *Oregon and California*, 426.

President James K. Polk and Senator Thomas Benton Hart: Brothers that Helped Claim the West

With so much praise bestowed on our first President and Brother, George Washington, the lesser known Presidents of the mystic tie tend to be over-shadowed. One who surely deserves more praise would be the eleventh President, James Knox Polk (1845–1849).[171] This Brother not only brought Oregon and California under the American flag, but also the Lone Star state of Texas.

> Polk's career was from first to last that of an honest, conscientious, and limited man, who was incapable perhaps of the highest moral elevation, but was certainly also incapable of deceit and double-dealing. He rose from step to step by a combination of plodding, careful industry and strict integrity.[172]

> The simple truth was, Polk wanted more territory. No president in American history had ever been so frank in his aims for seizing real estate; it was a curious time in the history of the settlement of North America, a time when the European powers, though fast losing their purchase on the New World, still held dreams of securing the last great unmapped chunks of a wild continent…. In this competitive environment, President Polk took the position that the United States should aggressively pursue its territorial interests now or else risk forfeiting them forever….Nearly from the moment he took office in 1845, Polk had seemed perfectly willing to fight two simultaneous wars-one with Mexico over Texas and California and another with Great Britain over Oregon.[173]

> …a great president. Said what he intended to do and did it.[174]

After his four years in office, brother Polk had increased the size of

---

171 Initiated Sept 4, 1820, in Columbia Lodge N⁰ 31 in Columbia, Tennessee. See Randall Rogers, *Our Masonic Presidents* (1998), 95.

172 Allan Nevins, *Polk: the Diary of a President, 1845–1849* (1929), xiv.

173 Sides, "Blood and Thunder," 55.

174 Letter to Dean Acheson (unsent), August 26, 1960. In Harry S Truman & Robert H. Ferrell, *Off the Record: The Private Papers of Harry S Truman* (New York: Harper & Row, 1980), 390.

1149

America by 522 million acres.[175] He obviously had a lot of help from other politicians, one of whom was Senator of Missouri, Thomas Hart Benton. Brother Benton[176] was equally if not more ambitious in extending the territory of the United States to the Pacific ocean as Polk was.

Brother Benton was truly the face and voice of the popular Manifest Destiny, a rally for an America that spanned from coast to coast. In the 1820s, he proposed a bill that created the building of the Santa Fe trail which opened up the southwest.[177] In the 1840s, he promoted his Son-in-Law,[178] John C. Frémont, to survey the substantial section of land between Missouri and Oregon Country.

Frémont's Wildest Tour of the West — May of 1845

After meeting with President Polk, Frémont left Washington with the understanding that California would become a part of the United States either through purchasing it or going to war with Mexico.[179] At the age of thirty-two and in charge of over fifty volunteers, Frémont headed west again but this time on the Santa Fe trail. Their first major stop was at Bent's Fort[180] located in modern day southeastern Colorado. Here Frémont sought and obtained Kit Carson's service yet again.[181]

The group crossed the Sierra Nevada Mountains with greater ease this time and set up camp in the San Joaquin Valley.[182] From here, Frémont went to Monterey where he met with General José Castro to explain why he was in Alta California. His explanation was that he and his 60 civilian assistants were simply conducting a survey of the territory—another scientific exploration for the United States. Castro approved of this for a time but eventually rumors started to circulate among the native Californios about Frémont's true intentions. Castro ended up losing his

---

175 Sides, "Blood and Thunder," 56.

176 A charter member of Missouri Lodge № 12. See Denslow, *Territorial Masonry* (1925), 56.

177 Sides, "Blood and Thunder," 61.

178 Frémont married Senator Benton's daughter, Jessie Benton, in 1841.

179 Sides, "Blood and Thunder," 87.

180 Established in 1833 by Charles and William Bent as well as Brother Ceran St. Vrain (Montezuma Lodge № 109 in New Mexico).

181 Hafen, *Mountain Men and the Fur Trade*, 179.

182 Robert M. Utley, *A Life Wild and Perilous* (New York: Henry Holt & Company, 1997), 231.

patience and ordered Frémont to leave the area immediately. Instead of leaving, Frémont defiantly ignored him and fortified himself in the local mountains.[183] Castro resorted to bringing his 200-man army and getting in a standoff with Frémont's group of 60.[184]

Fortunately before any guns were fired or blood spilled, Frémont came to his senses and agreed to leave the area. He and his men headed north into Oregon Country where they camped on the banks of Lake Klamath. One night as they were sleeping, local Indians infiltrated their camp and bludgeoned two of the French Voyageurs to death.[185] The following day, Frémont's men retaliated by burning the nearby Klamath encampments to the ground. While this type of violence has been portrayed often in Western films, the lesser-known fact is that there were also people during this time working hard to establish a civilized and decent society.

Just 200 miles north of Lake Klamath, a small American town was buzzing with activity. Thanks in part to the maps produced from Frémont's previous expeditions, a steady flow of emigrants had been making their way across the Oregon trail and settling at a place called Oregon City. It was in this town that plans were being made to start the first Masonic lodge in the Wild West.

Oregon City, the Cradle of Freemasonry in the Pacific Northwest: 1846[186]

As the fur trade died out for American trappers, many moved and settled down in the Willamette Valley[187] of Oregon. Perhaps the thought of

183 The Gabilan Mountains southeast of Monterey Bay, California.

184 Theodore Henry Hittell, *History of California* (San Francisco: N.J. Stone & Company, 1898), 2:415–19.

185 Charles John Frémont & Mosheim Samuel Smucker, *The Life of Colonel John Charles Frémont, and His Narrative of Explorations and Adventures, in Kansas, Nebraska, Oregon and California* (New York: Miller, Orton & Mulligan, 1856), 4:25.

186 The claim upon which Oregon City stands was taken up by Dr. John McLoughlin in 1829. In 1838, an American by the name of W.C. Remick built a cabin there and claimed proprietorship of the premises. Dr. McLoughlin bought him out to avoid any trouble with him. Oregon City was not only the site of the first Masonic meeting on the west coast, but also the first capital of a provisional government west of the Rockies. The first legislature met here on July 5, 1843. The first American flag was flown by the provisional government here in 1846. *Oregon Native Son and Historical Magazine*, Vol. 1, No. 4 (August 1899), 218.

187 South of modern day Portland.

returning to a normal life the States was unbearable after living in the wild for so long.[188] The remarks of one mountain man, Robert Newell, eloquently explains the attractions of Oregon Country:

> Come, we are done with this life in the mountains—done with the wading in beaver dams, and freezing or starving alternately-done with the Indian trading and Indian fighting. The fur trade is dead in the Rocky Mountains, and it is no place for us now, if it ever was. We are young yet, and have life before us. We cannot waste it here; we cannot or will not return to the States. Let us go down to the Willamette and take farms…. Shall we turn American settlers?[189]

By 1846, Oregon City was the terminus of the Oregon Trail and a thriving American settlement.[190] When emigrants arrived, they found a main street, three hotels, several dozen businesses,[191] four churches, one hundred houses, five sawmills, a newspaper, two flour mills, and a population just over one thousand souls.[192] Surprisingly it was Oregon—not California—that Americans increasingly viewed as the Promised Land where "plants and trees flower all winter…vegetable growth is enormous, where rain falls, or rivers run."[193]

The first major wagon train arrived in 1842 bringing over a dozen wagons and 107 emigrants. The next year was known as the 'Great Migration' as nearly one thousand emigrants came to Oregon Country along with

188 Some mountain men were highly valued based on their experience as mountain men, such as Kit Carson. Other mountain men returned to the States to work as guides for wagon parties crossing the Oregon Trail.

189 Victor, *The River of the West*, 264.

190 In 1844, Oregon City became the first American City incorporated west of the Rocky Mountains. *https://en.wikipedia.org/wiki/Oregon_City,_Oregon*.

191 Consisting of two taverns, one hatter, one tannery, three tailor shops, two cabinet makers, two silversmiths, one copper smith, two blacksmiths, one physician and three lawyers. See Joel Palmer, *Journal of Travels over the Rocky Mountains to the Mouth of the Columbia River; made during the years 1845 and 1846* (Cincinnati: J.A. & U.P. James, 1847), 76. One of these lawyers was soon to be brother Asa Lovejoy. One of the general merchandise stores owned by soon to be brother Captain John H. Couch. See *Oregon Native Son and Historical Magazine* (June 1899), 49.

192 Winther, *The Old Oregon Country*, 105. Also see Palmer, *Journal of Travels*, 76.

193 Archer Butler Hulbert, *The Call of the Columbia: Iron Men and the Saints Take the Oregon Trail* (Colorado Springs, Colo.: Stewart Commission of Colorado College and the Denver Public Library, 1934), 165.

700 cows. For John McLoughlin at Fort Vancouver, this must have been like watching a slow leak start to grow at the bottom of a very large dam. People came for a variety of reasons but a better quality of life was near the top. In 1844, a giant flood destroyed many farms and lives along the Missouri River. Even with natural disasters aside, a plethora of ailments such as measles, mumps, scarlet fever, dysentery, influenza, smallpox and cholera were spreading throughout American cities.[194] Improved health was one of the most common reasons people made the great migration.

In 1839, there were an estimated 100 Americans south of the Columbia River.[195] In 1843, the population was around 1,500, and by 1850 it had ballooned to over 13,000.[196] The majority of emigrants came from Kentucky, Illinois, Ohio and Missouri.[197]

"The fact is, this country is settled by a very steady people, a plain people, and it was settled by families; a very moral people as a rule."[198]

First Meeting to Discuss Forming a Lodge

In the bustling town built at the base of Willamette Falls, a tiny newspaper was in circulation called the *Oregon Spectator*[199]. On February the 5th, 1846, while Frémont was in the Sierra Nevada mountains, a tiny ad ran in the newspaper which read:

---

194 William A. Bowen, *The Willamette Valley, Migration and Settlement on the Oregon Frontier* (Seattle: University of Washington Press, 1978), 18-19.

195 Forty-eight percent of the population were less than eighteen years old and of this, seventy-eight percent were under twelve years old. Only seven percent of the population was over forty-five. Sixty percent were male. See Bowen, *The Willamette Valley*, 13.

196 Winther, *The Old Oregon Country*, 100.

197 Origin of Oregonians in 1850: 18% from Missouri, 8% from Illinois, 7% from Ohio, 6% from Kentucky. See Bowen, *The Willamette Valley*, 18–19.

198 Solomon Zumwalt, *The Biography of Adam Zumwalt* (Berkeley, Calif.: Bancroft Library, University of California), 16.

199 *The Oregon Spectator* was the first newspaper printed on the west coast. *Oregon Native Son and Historical Magazine*, Vol. 1, No. 4 (August, 1899), 218. In 1844, the Oregon Printing Association was formed and George Abernethy went to New York to purchase a printing press. The very first printing of the newspaper was Februrary 5, 1846, which included the Masonic notice. See Palmer, *Journal of Travels*, 171.

A. Lawrence Lovejoy,

Attorney and Counsellor at Law and Solicitor in Chancery.

WILL practice in the Supreme and Criminal Courts of Oregon territory, and in the several County Courts.

Office, corner of Main and Second streets.

Oregon City, Jan. 20, 1846. 1y1

Masonic Notice.

THE members of the MASONIC FRATERNITY in Oregon Territory, are respetfully requested to meet at the City Hotel, in Oregon City, on the 21st inst., to adopt some measures to obtain a charter for a lodge.

JOSEPH HULL,
P. G. STEWART,
WM. P. DOUGHERTY.

Febuary 5, 1846.

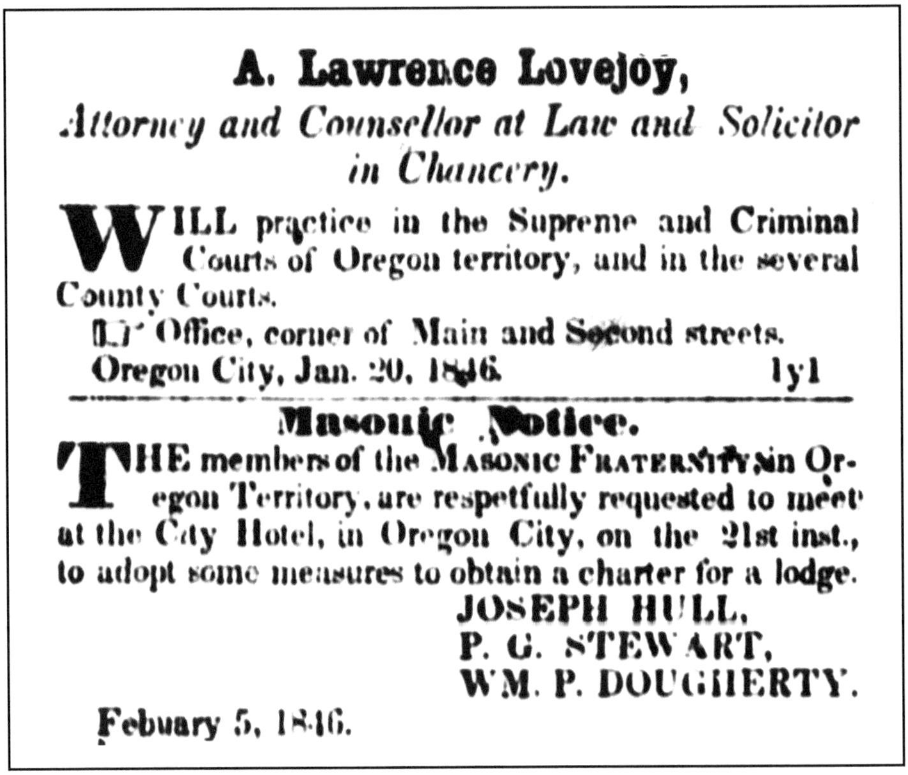

Masonic Notice in the *Oregon Spectator* of Feb. 5, 1846.

Masonic Notice.

The members of the MASONIC FRATERNITY in Oregon Territory, are respectfully requested to meet at the City Hotel in Oregon City, on the 21st inst., to adopt some measures to obtain a charter for a lodge.

[Signed] Joseph Hull[200]
P.G. Stewart
Wm. P. Dougherty[201]

200 Joseph Hull, Past Master of Milford Lodge № 54 in Milford, Ohio. He left Oregon for the California gold rush. Born on January 24, 1813 in Steubenville, Ohio. He died in San Diego on January 4, 1896 and was buried in Los Angeles. See Frank Knoll, *How Masonry Came to Oregon*, 18, and Edwin Allen Sherman, *Fifty Years of Masonry in California*, 2:47.

201 M. John Hodson, H. William Upton, W. Jonas Brown, & Cornelius Hedges, *Masonic History of the Northwest: A Graphical Recital of the Organization and Growth of Freemasonry in the North West States* (San Francisco, Calif.: History Publishing Company, 1902), 265.

This ad caught the attention of a few brethren in the area, who assembled at the hotel to sign a petition for a charter. These brothers were Joseph Hull, Peter G. Stewart, William P. Dougherty, Fendal Cason, Leon A. Smith, Frederick Waymier and Lot Whitcombe. Peter G. Stewart suggested the name Multnomah Lodge[202] (referring to the original name of the Willamette River when brother William Clark explored it forty years prior).[203]

With the petition drafted and signed, it was given to a man named Joel Palmer who was on his way back to Cincinnati to retrieve his family. Mr. Palmer was not yet a Mason, but later became one after he returned and settled down near Oregon City.[204] In order to establish the first Masonic lodge in the far west, the petition would have to be hand delivered to the Grand Lodge of Missouri over 2,000 miles away.

202 Hodson, Upton, Brown & Hedges, *Masonic History of the Northwest*, 266.

203 Lewis and Clark Journal, April 2, 1806 Also see Palmer, *Journal of Travels*, 78.

204 Joel Palmer was later a member of Lafayette Lodge Nº 3. Hodson, Upton, Brown & Hedges, *Masonic History of the Northwest*, 266

1845 *to* 1850

The Oregon Trail
and the First
Masonic Charter
West of the Rockies

JOEL PALMER arrived at Oregon City in November of 1845, having spent the previous seven months crossing the Oregon Trail.[1] He was beyond pleased to have made it to the buzzing town of 600 residents. Unimproved lots were available for one to five hundred dollars and most already sold to retiring HBC employees.[2] Palmer had come to the region to find a suitable location to make a claim for his family to settle at in the coming year. Surprisingly, he had to look for some time and at considerable distance from Oregon City to find a claim.[3] All of the land south of the city had already been claimed, settled and improved.[4] To completely avoid this early sprawl, some pioneers like Bro. Michael Troutman Simmons simply went where no one else dared to go.

Brother Michael Simmons, the first American to settle on the Puget Sound: 1845

At age thirty, Michael Simmons left Missouri with a large wagon train. As was the custom for large wagon parties, an election was held to determine who would be in charge of the wagon party. Subsequently Mr. Simmons was elected Colonel, or second in command. He successfully lead his wagon train to Oregon Country where he and a smaller group decided against taking a claim south of the Columbia River. Defying John McLoughlin's wishes,[5] they went up the Cowlitz River and then to the Puget Sound. By this time there was a well established portage road from the Cowlitz River thanks to the Hudson's Bay Company.[6]

After reaching the HBC post of Fort Nisqually[7], Simmons was told

1   Palmer, *Journal of Travels*, 76.

2   Palmer, *Journal of Travels*, 77.

3   The settlement started with one building in 1840 and was joined by five or six others in the spring of 1843. It then exploded after the "great migration" with seventy five homes by December of 1843. The value of Oregon City real estate grew by over 300% during these months. See James R. Gibson, *Farming the Frontier: The Agricultural Opening of the Oregon Country, 1786-1846* (Seattle: University of Washington Press, 1985), 131.

4   Palmer, *Journal of Travels*, 80.

5   It is speculated that because of racial discrimination against one member of Simmons' party, they were barred from settling south of the Columbia River. See Ficken, *Washington Territory*, 6.

6   Herbert Hunt & Floyd C. Washington, *West of the Cascades: Historical and Descriptive; the Explorers, the Indians, the Pioneers, the Modern*, (1917), 1:29.

7   Built in 1832 near the present town of Dupont, Washington. It was operated by

Michael Simmons. c. 1844
Aldrich Photo Studios, Washington State Historical Society

about a nearby location suitable for settlement.[8] At this designated site, Simmons built a mill and established "New Market[9]" in October of 1845.[10]

Olympia established by a Mason: 1846

Just one year later a few miles north of Simmons site, Bro. Edmund

Scottish, Native Americans, Hawaiian Kanakas, French-Canadians, Metis, West Indians, Englishman and later Americans. It became a major agricultural hub for the Hudson's Bay Company under the Puget Sound Agricultural Company. See Galbraith, John S, "The British and Americans at Fort Nisqually, 1846-1859," The Pacific Northwest Quarterly, University of Washington, (1950), 41

8   Ibid.

9   New Market later became Tumwater, Washington.

10 Gordon R. Newell, *So Fair A Dwelling Place: A History of Olympia and Thurston County, Washington* (Olympia, Wash.: G.R. Newell, 1950), 2–7.

Sylvester and Mr. Levi Smith staked a claim on an even better section of land and called it Olympia.[11] Plats in this claim were quickly sold and for a time it was "*the* town on the sound."

Slowly but surely, pioneers were discovering the rich farm lands up for grabs around the Puget Sound. With good health and a strong work ethic, one could do quite well for oneself in Oregon Country. Within a decade even Olympia was brushed aside as a new town on the Sound was established. This one was fifty miles to the north and featured a large, deep bay, access to a fertile valley[12] and an established Indian settlement. The town of course was Seattle[13] and it would be named after a local Duwamish Chief of the same name who Brother[14] David Swinson Maynard[15] named his store[16] after. For the pioneers arriving in the late 1840s, "North

11 Currently the Capital of Washington State. See Ibid.

12 The valley which starts at the Port of Seattle and goes through Georgetown, Tukwila, Kent, Auburn, Pacific and Sumner, Washington.

13 Seattle was officially named on the 23rd of May, 1853, when David S. Maynard individually filed a plat and Carson D. Boren and Arthur A. Denny unitedly filed another plat of adjoining parts of their three claims, they each so calling the place they were then engaged in planning and preparing for. See Thomas W. Prosch, *David S. Maynard and Catherine T. Maynard: Biographies of Two of the Oregon Immigrants of 1850* (Seattle: Lowman & Hanford, 1906), 36. Also see Arthur Denny, *Pioneer Days on Puget Sound* (Seattle: C.B. Bagley, 1888), 21.

14 Maynard was a member of St. John's Lodge Nº 9 in Seattle, Washington. He was elected for membership on November 29, 1860, indicating he probably hailed originally from a lodge in Ohio. Obtained from the Membership Record of St. John's Lodge Nº 9 on August 16, 2016.

15 Maynard arrived at Alki beach on March 31, 1852, with Chief Seattle who had told him about the area being good for fishing. Initially Dr. Maynard planned to temporarily pack salmon for export to San Francisco but ended up becoming a permanent resident. See Arthur Denny, *Pioneer Days on Puget Sound* (Seattle: C.B. Bagley, 1888), 18. The following spring, (Freemason) Captain William Renton arrived at Alki point where he built a lumber mill temporarily before relocating to Port Blakely. He later became an important proprietor of coal mining and has the distinction of having Renton, Washington, named after him. See Denny, *Pioneer Days*, 38

Maynard would be the first professional man, first doctor, first pharmacist, first official, first employer, first real estate seller, first merchant, the first in and of a great number of movements and undertakings of business, social, and public character in the city of Seattle. See Prosch, *David S. Maynard and Catherine T. Maynard*, 62.

16 A log structure called "The Seattle Exchange" which Maynard lived in and sold medicine, groceries, tools and clothing out of. It stood on the present "Northwest corner of First Avenue and Main Street" in Pioneer Square, Seattle. See Prosch, *David S. Maynard and Catherine T. Maynard*, 28.

State of Affairs for Americans settled in Oregon Country

By the early 1840s there were already two failed attempts to pass a bill through Congress for territorial representation of Oregon, one in 1838 and another in 1841. Instead of waiting for regular American laws and regulations which would occur under a U.S. Territory, settlers in Oregon Country adopted their own set of laws that lasted from 1841 to 1848.[1]

1 Dorothy O. Johansen, *Empire of the Columbia, 2nd Edition* (New York: Harper & Row, 1967), 184–94.

Oregon," particularly on the Puget Sound, was the favored place in which to settle as opposed to the crowded Willamette Valley.

Fortunately for American emigrants, the tug of war between the U.S. and Great Britain over the territory would come to an end in 1846, when the Treaty of Oregon was signed. Brother and President James Polk would get his wish with this treaty, bringing into the United States all the land encompassing modern day Oregon, Washington, Idaho, and Montana.

With territorial recognition from the United States came tremendous benefits to the settlers in Oregon. The dam that John McLoughlin had seen a crack in was now about to burst wide open.

Joel Palmer visits Fort Vancouver: 1845

After completing a thorough survey of the area around Oregon City, Joel Palmer visited John McLoughlin at Fort Vancouver. He like many Americans before him, found McLoughlin to be "much of a gentleman" and hospitable during his visit.[17] He entered through a gate in the twelve-foot-high timber wall surrounding the fort and to his surprise, observed many of the HBC employees ranting, frolicking and gambling about the grounds. It was, after all, Christmas Day when Palmer chose to visit the fort.[18]

On board a nearby ship, sailors were partying late into the night and

17 Palmer, *Journal of Travels*, 99.
18 Palmer, *Journal of Travels*, 98.

were so "gloriously drunk" upon paddling in to shore, one of them fell out of the boat, and his friends were barely able to pull him back up.[19] It was in this celebratory atmosphere that Palmer got his first impression of Hudson's Bay Company. He learned that it had been a long standing custom of officials at Fort Vancouver to discourage American settlement north of the Columbia River.[20] Palmer suspected that the warm welcome McLouglin gave him was actually just to encourage him to stay south of the Columbia. With his time running out, Palmer never made it to the Puget Sound to see it personally. He did however, make a startlingly accurate prediction about the region's potential.

> The excellent harbors of Puget's sound, with its many advantages, and the delightful country about it, are sufficient to induce capitalists to look that way. This will probably be the principal port upon the coast. Here will doubtless be our navy yard and shipping stores.—Joel Palmer, 1847[21]

Palmer talked about Fort Nisqually in his journal but it is unlikely that he new about Simmon's recent settlement there. Perhaps HBC was withholding this information to not bring extra attention to the Puget Sound. Nonetheless, Palmer was satisfied with his visit and returned to the States.

Palmer returns to the States and Delivers the Petition: March 1846

In early March before the rivers got too high, Palmer and an unnamed partner pushed off from the banks at Oregon City. Palmer had really grown to enjoy the people and the atmosphere in Oregon Country during the time he had spent there. Though he did not make mention it in his journal, Palmer had with him the handwritten petition from the brothers of Oregon City along with other mail being returned to the States.

After a few hours of paddling down the Willamette River, they stopped at the newly-platted town of Portland.[22] Here Palmer noted the potential

---

19 Palmer, *Journal of Travels*, 99.

20 Palmer, *Journal of Travels*, 100.

21 Palmer, *Journal of Travels*, 101.

22 Unsurprisingly, they stopped due to heavy rains which prevented their progress onto the Columbia. In the town of Portland, they roomed with a man named Mr. Bell.

John Mix Stanley (1814–1872). Fort Nez Perces.
Engraving, 1853. Library of Congress.

of the claim saying, "this will probably be a town of some consequence, as it occupies a handsom site, and is at the head of ship navigation."[23] Of course, the town would eventually become a metropolis,[24] but Portland was only three years old in 1845. It had been settled by a Mr. Asa Lovejoy[25] and William Overton. Lovejoy would coincidentally be one of the first candidates initiated into Multnomah Lodge when the charter was returned.

The following morning they paddled to the mouth of the Willamette

Joel Palmer, *Journal of Travels Over the Rocky Mountains* (Cincinnati: J.A. & U.P. James, 1847), 107.

23 Palmer, *Journal of Travels*, 107.

24 Growth was slow at first for Portland. One year after staking his 320 acre claim there, Overton sold out to F.W. Pettygrove for $50 who then built the first log cabin there. By 1849 there were only one hundred residents in this small settlement. By 1851, when the town was incorporated, the population was 1,000. Today over two million people live in the Portland metro area and it is the 26th most populated metro area in America. *http://en.wikipedia.org/wiki/List_of_United_States_cities_by_population.* Also see Palmer, *Journal of Travels*, 172.

25 Born in Groton, Massachusetts, on March 14, 1808. Went to Cambridge where he studied law and subsequently passed the bar. Came across the Oregon trail in 1842 with Dr. Elijah White. After many detours along the way, he arrived in Oregon City in November of 1843 where he opened a law practice. *Oregon Native Son and Historical Magazine*, (June 1899), 48.

and then turned up the Columbia River as far as they could before they had to pull in to shore to rest. The site they chose to beach at was upon the mouth of a river[26] where they found the remnants of brother Michael Simmons camp from a year earlier.[27]

Was Palmer aware of the rich and recent history on the Columbia River? Did he marvel at how the Astorians had just settled there thirty-five years prior? Its more likely he was just trying to cover as much ground as he could rather than reflecting on the romantic history of the area. After ten days of paddling they reached the Dalles where they pulled their boat into shore and exchanged it for horses.[28]

Palmer's next stop was over one hundred miles away at the HBC-owned Fort Nez Perce. Here, he camped along side a large group of Nez Perce Indians.[29] From Fort Nez Perce, they followed the Walla Walla River to Dr. Marcus Whitman's mission. Whitman, as the reader may recall, was at the 1835 rendezvous with Kit Carson and now, eleven years later, was quite busy running his mission. Not only did he have many affairs to manage with the local Cayuse Indians, but his mission sat right on the Oregon Trail and thus attracted a constant stream of American emigrants. The date of Palmer's arrival to Whitman's mission was March 28th, 1846.[30]

Little could anyone know that on November 29th of the following year, Marcus Whitman, his wife, and eleven others would be slain at this very site by Cayuse Indians. Additionally "about 50 survivors are held hostage for a month and then ransomed by the Hudson's Bay Company. The attack, a pivotal event in Northwest history, will lead to a war of re-taliation against the Cayuse and the extension of federal control over the present-day states of Washington, Oregon, Idaho, and parts of Montana and Wyoming."[31] But for now, all was well. After a few days rest at the

26 The Washougal River of Clarke County, Washington. "A number of immigrants had stopped here in 1844 to establish their winter camp, going on the next year to settle at Puget Sound." Palmer, *Journal of Travels*, 179.

27 Palmer, *Journal of Travels*, 107.

28 The Dalles is one of the oldest continually inhabited sites in North America392 and for good reason. The Dalles is a series of waterfalls on the Columbia River where Indians were able to rely on regular schools of salmon accumulating at the falls. Thanks to this predictable food source, they were able to live there or nearby for millennia.

29 Palmer, *Journal of Travels*, 109.

30 Palmer, *Journal of Travels*, 111.

31 Palmer, *Journal of Travels*, 111,

mission, Palmer continued onwards to their next stop at Spalding's Mission.

Henry Harmon Spalding was another prominent missionary in the Pacific Northwest at the time. Spalding and his wife Eliza had split off from Marcus Whitman and established their own mission on the Snake River near the modern day border of Washington and Idaho.[32] Here Palmer's party stayed for a week taking in many stories from Spalding's colorful life. You can almost imagine Palmer and Spalding sitting across from each other enjoying a cup of coffee as Spalding told his greatest stories from the previous decade in the Wild West. Spalding had come west ten years earlier with an American Fur Company supply train.[33] Imagine how hard it was just to get to the region not to mention building up and maintaining a mission in the heart of Indian country.

Missions and their Effect on Indigenous Peoples

Unlike Whitman's Mission, Spalding chose to build his in a more secluded location off the beaten trail. As a result, the local Indians were fascinated by Palmer's party and were said to have "flocked in from all quarters" when he first arrived.[34] These were interesting times in the Pacific Northwest.

No matter where missionaries settled in the territory, it was a monumental task to influence local Indians to change their long established customs. But one thing that was almost universally understood was that white people usually had interesting items with them to trade.[35]

Perhaps this is why so many Indians came to the mission when Palmer arrived. The tribe had previously indicated their frustration to Spalding about the lack of trade goods coming through the area. In fact, they went so far as to say that if Spalding failed to increase the traffic of American trade goods through their land then he would need to leave.[36]

To the tribes of the upper plateau region, trading was a central part of life and as a result of this fact, American emigrants would be tolerated for a time. However, as the waves of emigrants grew larger and larger with

---

32 Joseph Gaston, *The Centennial History of Oregon, 1811–1911* (Chicago: S.J. Clarke Pub. Co., 1912), 1:255.

33 Hafen, *Mountain Men and the Fur Trade*, 244.

34 Palmer, *Journal of Travels*, 113.

35 Popular items included gunpowder, blankets, beads, tobacco, knives, and cooking utensils.

36 Palmer, *Journal of Travels*, 115.

Alfred Jacob Miller (1810–1874). *Fort Laramie.*
Watercolor on paper, c. 1858. Joslyn Art Museum, Omaha, Nebraska

each passing year, Indians started to see more consequences than benefits to their presence. They did not appear to care if people simply passed through their land, but if along the way they scared all the wild game then understandably this became a great concern for the Indians. From Palmer's journey in 1845, we have these remarkable notes from an Indian Chief:

a long while ago, some white chiefs passed up the Missouri, through my country, saying they were the red man's friends, and that as the red man found them, so would he find all the other pale faces. This country belongs to the red man, but his white brethren travels through, shooting the game and scaring it away. Thus the Indian loses all that he depends on to support his wives and children. The children of the red man cry for food, but there is none. But on the other hand, the Indian profits by the trade with the white man. Before the white man came, the game was tame, and easily caught, with the bow and arrow. Now the white man has frightened it, and the red man must go to the mountains. The red man needed long guns.[37]

37 Palmer, *Journal of Travels*, 25.

Alfred Jacob Miller (1810–1874). *Loading on Horseback-Buffalo swimming the Platte.* Pen and ink with sepia wash on paper. Beinecke Rare Book and Manuscript Library, Yale University, New Haven, Connecticut.

Palmer Reaches Fort Boise: April 29, 1846

In mid-April, Palmer returned to Whitman's mission to make his final arrangements before starting the big journey back to St. Louis. On April 17, Palmer—along with a group of 18 other people and 51 horses—left from Whitman's mission bound for the States.[38] They passed through knee deep snow in the Wind River Mountains before coming out on the other side nearly two weeks later. On the 29th of April they reached the Hudson's Bay Company trading post of Fort Boise near the confluence of the Snake and Boise Rivers.[39] Here they found a modest post in comparison to the vast enterprise of Fort Vancouver. However, a fort was a fort and they were grateful to be provided with fresh milk and butter.[40]

Palmer now found himself in the barren Snake River country, the desolate landscape which had brought Mr. Hunt's overland party to their knees years before. Unfortunately times had changed for the Shoshone peoples, they no longer saw novelty in white men passing through their country. In an attempt to threaten Palmer's party, Shoshone warriors lined up on a ridge overlooking Palmer's party and let out a series of terrifying

38 Palmer, *Journal of Travels*, 116.
39 "Location of Fort Boise, 1834–1855 (Fur Trade)." *Idaho State Historical Society Reference Series*, Number 29.
40 Palmer, *Journal of Travels*, 117.

screams while thrusting muskets, bows and arrows in the air.[41] Luckily, the Shoshones were just giving a warning this time. Eight years later, the Shoshones would attack a wagon train and kill nineteen American pioneers.[42]

Through South Pass and into Buffalo Country: May 26, 1846

Having safely made it through the Snake River region, Palmer's group was now crossing the continental divide through South Pass. The landscape would transform before their eyes with new wildlife such as buffalo, grizzly bears, big horn sheep, and antelopes.[43] The hunters in their group were quickly put to work and brought down a few buffalo.

Once they reached the Platte River[44] in Central Wyoming, the amount of buffalo increased dramatically. Palmer noted that the plains were "literally covered with buffalo, tens of thousands were to be seen at one view; antelope and black-tailed deer were seen in great abundance, and a few elk and common deer. One panther, and hundreds of wolves were also seen."[45]

What a breathtaking sight it must have been to see the "American Serengeti" in its virgin state. Yet as exciting as the wildlife was, nothing was more exhilarating than spotting the first stream of wagon trains that went on for miles.[46] After camping with this group of emigrants, Palmer

---

41 Palmer, *Journal of Travels*, 118.

42 Donald Shannon, *The Boise Massacre on the Oregon Trail: Attack on the Ward Party in 1854 and Massacres of 1859* (Caldwell, Idaho: Snake Country Pub., 2004).

43 Palmer, *Journal of Travels*, 119.

44 The Platte River was dangerous during the Oregon trail days before it was dammed in several locations in the twentieth century. It was very sensitive to the amount of rain and snow melt in the Rockies which fed it and as a result could rise and fall dramatically. It could rise while a large wagon party thought it was safe to cross or surprise a party camping on its banks in the middle if night with a flash flood. Additionally it was the main water source for the game which lived on the plains in this area so it attracted both emigrants and buffalo. See Rinker Buck, *The Oregon Trail: A New American Journey* (New York: Simon & Schuster, 2015), 131.

45 Palmer, *Journal of Travels*, 248.

46 This party consisted of 541 wagons, each containing an average of five people. Palmer, *Journal of Travels*, 120 & 181. Later estimates put the actual number of emigrants closer to 2,000 people. In this large wagon train were the ill-fated Donner Party of which 39 of the 87 in it would lose their lives to starvation and hypothermia. Additionally in this party was the first duly authenticated Mason to cross the plains to California: Bro. James Frazier Reed. (Sherman, *Fifty Years of Masonry in California*, 1:51).

Alfred Jacob Miller. *Caravan on the Platte. c. 1858*
Watercolor on paper. Joslyn Art Museum, Omaha, NE

and company were able to catch up on news from the States. Since Palmer had left Ohio a year before, he hadn't seen or heard anything from his wife and kids let alone what was happening with the country.[47]

Crossing paths with a large Wagon Party: June 5, 1846

How much we take for granted today the fact that we can get instant notifications on our smart phones with up to the minute news from around the globe. On June 5, 1846, the first Pony Express was still a decade away and the electrical telegraph only went as far west as St. Louis. All communications between the United States and Oregon Country were limited to travel by land over the Oregon Trail or by ship using the Isthmus of Panama.[48]

One interesting development that Palmer would have learned about was that the United States was now at war with Mexico.[49] This was of no concern to Palmer as he was focused on bringing his family back to

47 Palmer, *Journal of Travels*, 120,

48 The Isthmus of Panama is the narrow strip of land that lies between the Caribbean Sea and the Pacific Ocean, linking North and South America.

49 M. William Paxton, *Annals of Platte County, Missouri* (1837), 76. In March of 1846, Mexico declared war against the United States.

Oregon where he had plenty of things more important to focus on.

In one of the wagons that Palmer passed on the plains was a man named Francis Parkman who happened to be keeping a journal as well. Through his writings we are given another wonderful glimpse of the Oregon Trail:

> The level of monotony of the plain was unbroken as far as the eye could reach. Sometimes it glared in the sun, an expanse of hot, bare sand; sometimes it was veiled by long coarse grass. Skulls and whitening bones of buffalo were scattered everywhere; the ground was tracked by myriads of them, and often covered with the circular indentations where the bulls had wallowed in the hot weather. From every gorge and ravine, opening from the hills, descended deep, well-worn paths, where the buffalo issue twice a day in regular procession to drink in the Platte. The river itself runs through the midst, a thin sheet of rapid, turbid water, half a mile wide and scarcely two feet deep.[50]

> Sometimes I surprised shaggy old (buffalo) bulls grazing alone, or sleeping behind the ridges I ascended. They would leap up at my approach, stare stupidly at me through their tangled manes, and then gallop heavily away. The antelope were very numerous; and as they are always bold when in the neighborhood of buffalo, they would approach to look at me, gaze intently with their great round eyes, then suddenly leap aside, and stretch lightly away over the prairie, as swiftly as a racehorse. Squalid, ruffian-like wolves sneaked through the hollows and sandy ravines. Several times I passed through villages of prairie-dogs, who sat, each at the mouth of his burrow, holding his paws before him in a supplicating attitude, and yelping away most vehemently, whisking his little tail with every squeaking cry he uttered. Prairie-dogs are not fastidious in their choice of companions; various long checkered snakes were sunning themselves in the midst of the village, and demure little gray owls, with a large white ring around each eye, were perched side by side with the rightful inhabitants. The prairie teemed with life.... I noticed insects wholly different from any of the varieties found farther to the eastward. Gaudy butterflies fluttered about my horse's head; strangely formed beetles, glittering with metallic lustre, were crawling

50 Parker, *The Oregon Trail*, 62.

Pilgrims on the Plains. A.R. Waud & A. Bobbett.
Wood engraving, c. 1871. Library of Congress.

upon plants that I had never seen before; multitudes of lizards, too, were darting like lightning over the sand.[51]

It is worth noticing that on the Platte one may sometimes see the shattered wrecks of ancient claw-footed tables, well waxed and rubbed, or massive bureaus of carved oak. These, some of them no doubt the relics of ancestral prosperity in the colonial time, must have encountered strange vicissitudes. Brought, perhaps, originally from England; then, with the declining fortunes of their owners, borne across the Allegheny Mountains to the wilderness of Ohio or Kentucky; then to Illinois or Missouri; and now at last fondly stowed away in the family wagon for the interminable journey to Oregon. But the stern privations of the way are little anticipated. The cherished relic is soon flung out to scorch and crack upon the hot prairie.[52]

Another group present in this large wagon train was the ill-fated

51   Parker, *The Oregon Trail*, 77.
52   Parker, *The Oregon Trail*, 83.

Donner party. These emigrants would suffer terribly in a storm while trying to cross the Sierra Nevada mountains. Brother James Frazier Reed, who would go on to sign the petition for San Jose Lodge Nº 10, was a survivor of this party.[53]

Petition arrives in St. Joseph, Missouri: July 7, 1846

It took four months for Palmer and company to get from Oregon City to St. Joseph, Missouri. The mixture of relief and exhaustion must have been beyond words. They spent their first night at a mission where they were able to take hot baths and shave for the first time since leaving Oregon. Palmer said that even though they had just spent the previous several months together, they could hardly recognize each other with their new, cleaned-up look.[54]

No longer were they in danger of Indian attacks which required watchmen to be on constant alert around the clock. They were now back in the safety of the United States where they could all disperse freely in their own direction. It is interesting to note that while they were relieved to be back in the states, the political climate they had returned to was surely scorching! The United States had recently declared war against Mexico and needed 50,000 volunteers to fight on the front lines.[55]

With all the happenings, there were no newspaper reporters nor cannon ball salutes to greet Palmer's party as they returned to civilization. It is more likely they just slipped right through the city unnoticed and planned their next steps. First and most importantly, Palmer had to get to Cincinnati to reunite with his family.[56] Secondly, he needed to deliver the mail he brought with him which contained the petition for a Masonic Lodge. The letter which contained the petition was addressed to Brother James A. Spratt in Platte City, Missouri.[57] Fortunately Platte City was only a short steamboat ride downriver from St. Joseph.[58]

---

53 O. Leon Whitsell, *One Hundred Years of Freemasonry in California* (San Francisco: Grand Lodge, Free and Accepted Masons in California, 1950), 47.

54 Palmer, *Journal of Travels*, 124.

55 Paxton, M. William. 1837. Annals of Platte County, Missouri. 77

56 Palmer, *Journal of Travels*, 125.

57 Member of Platte City Lodge Nº 56 and likely an attorney at Platte City. See Paxton, *Annals of Platte County*, 59—citing a "J.G. Spratt" as an attorney registered in Platte City in 1844–1846.

58 From Platte City, Palmer continued on to St. Louis and then boarded another ship

Missouri in the 1840s

- The total number of members of Platte City Lodge № 56 in 1846 was 27.
- Total number of Masonic lodges in Missouri in 1846: 57.[1]
- Total number of active Masons belonging to Grand Lodge of Missouri lodges: 1,135.
- Though Platte City was willing to sponsor the petition for Multnomah Lodge, they were considered a delinquent lodge after missing their Grand Lodge dues in 1845 and 1846 in the amount of $58.[2]
- It took twenty days for news to reach Platte City from Washington, D.C.
- The population of St. Louis at this time was only 28,354 people.[3]
- The population of the United States was 17,069,453 in 1840.[4]
- The population of Missouri was 383,702 in 1840.
- The winter of 1843 was the coldest on record with six inches of snow on the ground in Platte County.
- By March many are staging at Westport to cross the Oregon Trail.
- In June of 1844 the Missouri River floods at record highs, St. Louis is under seven feet of water.[5]
- With the flooding comes sickness, many people catch the "fever" and die.
- Mexican war of 1846 causes boom in Platte City economy as agriculture prices skyrocket.[6]

1   *Proceedings of the Grand Lodge of the State of Missouri, Convened in the City of St. Louis, Oct 12, 1846* (St. Louis: Keenle & Field, 1846), 44.
2   *Proceedings of the Grand Lodge of the State of Missouri, Convened in the City of St. Louis, Oct 12, 1846* (St. Louis: Keenle & Field, 1846), 40.
3   Paxton, Annals of Platte County, 52.
4   Paxton, Annals of Platte County, 123.
5   Paxton, Annals of Platte County, 123.
6   Paxton, Annals of Platte County, 82.

Though he made no mention of it in his journal, the simple petition that Palmer had brought with him from Oregon was in effect the great spark for Freemasonry in the Pacific Northwest. It is impressive to consider that this one piece of paper would help form the first Masonic lodge in the Oregon Territory. Nearly seven generations later that same territory contains two Grand Lodges and over five hundred individual lodges across Oregon and Washington State.[59] To take it one step further, every man who has been made a Mason in Oregon or Washington State can trace his Masonic lineage back to this piece of paper which made its way overland thanks to Joel Palmer.[60]

Platte City Lodge No. 56

The small town of Platte city originated as a mill built on the banks of waterfall, just like Oregon City.[61] The mill was built in 1837 and it slowly attracted settlers who cleared the surrounding land and developed it into a small town.

Seemingly all at once, in 1842 the town got its first newspaper, attorneys, physicians,[62] and a Masonic lodge.[63] Additionally Platte City was incorporated that year and one of the signers for the petition for incorporation was the same William Dougherty whose signature was now found on the petition for a Masonic Lodge in Oregon City.[64]

to Cincinnati, Ohio. From Cincinnati he took a stagecoach to Laurel, Indiana, where he reunited with his wife and children. Imagine the scene as Palmer's stage pulled up to his home and his wife came running out to greet him. He had been gone for a year and a quarter with zero contact between he and his family. Palmer sold the notes from his trip to a publisher in Cincinnati who printed them as a helpful guide for Oregon Trail migrants. The book went on to become a much used guide book and printed in four editions.

59 There have been over three hundred lodges chartered in Washington and over two hundred in Oregon.

60 The first Masonic lodge meeting would be held in Oregon City in 1848 after Pierre Barlow Cornwall returned the charter.

61 Paxton, *Annals of Platte County*, 19.

62 One of these doctors, a man by the name of Dr. N.M. Shrock (lived October 5, 1810 to March 25, 1852) was known to be an "enthusiastic Mason who organized the formation of Platte City Lodge N⁰ 56. He was well informed in the mysteries of Masonry, and with diligence instructed his brethren." Paxton, *Annals of Platte County*, 49 & 147.

63 Granted dispensation on June of 1842. Grand Lodge of Missouri, *Proceedings of 1842 Session*, 8.

64 Paxton, *Annals of Platte County*, 47.

E. Sachse, *View of St. Louis from Lucas Place.*
Lithograph, 1854. Missouri History Museum, St. Louis, Missouri.

William P. Dougherty had lived in Platte City sometime between 1842 and 1845, and joined Platte City Lodge prior to heading west for Oregon City.[65] Dougherty was both a fraternal brother and business acquaintance of Bro. James A. Spratt in Platte City. Through this connection, a proper connection was made to get the petition to the Grand Lodge of Missouri.

Petition Presented to Grand Lodge: October 17, 1846

The petition and letter accompanying it were read by Platte City Lodge № 56 which endorsed the request by the Oregon City brothers. Brothers from Platte City Lodge then sent the petition on to St. Louis where it was delivered to the Grand Lodge.[66] There are no records of any members of Platte City Lodge being present at that year's Grand Lodge session.[67]

65 "Merchants located at Platte City, as of January, 1841: G.W. Dougherty, W.H. Spratt, J.H. Spratt." Paxton, *Annals of Platte County,* 42.

66 Hodson, Upton, Brown & Hedges, *Masonic History of the Northwest,* 266. Also see *Proceedings of the Grand Lodge of the State of Missouri Convened in the City of St. Louis. Oct 12, 1846* (St. Louis: Keenle & Field, 1847), 18.

67 Members, representatives and delegates indicate that no brothers from Platte City Lodge were present. *Proceedings of the Grand Lodge of the State of Missouri. Convened*

Saint Louis in 1855. Leopold Gast and Brother. c. 1855.
Lithograph on stone. Library of Congress.

The Grand Lodge met for five solid days before the petition from the Oregon City brothers was read. Finally, on Saturday, October 17, 1846, exactly two hundred and thirty nine days since the brothers had drafted it in Oregon City, the petition was read and referred to the committee on applications.[68] The following Monday, October 19, the committee chairman, William Humphreys, recommended that the Most Worshipful Grand Master grant the brethren of Oregon Territory a charter in accordance with the ancient regulations of the fraternity.[69]

With the Grand Master's blessing, a charter was printed for Multnomah Lodge № 84 and appeared in the proceedings.[70] Platte City Lodge had its own Worshipful Master, H.B. Callahan, bring the charter from Saint Louis back to Platte City.[71] Now the charter just needed to get back across the two thousand miles of terrain to Oregon City.

in the City of St. Louis. Oct 12, 1846 (St. Louis: Keenle & Field, 1847), 43.

68 *Proceedings of the Grand Lodge of the State of Missouri. Convened in the City of St. Louis. Oct 12, 1846* (St. Louis: Keenle & Field, 1847), 18.

69 *Proceedings of the Grand Lodge of the State of Missouri. Convened in the City of St. Louis. Oct 12, 1846* (St. Louis: Keenle & Field, 1847), 23.

70 *Proceedings of the Grand Lodge of the State of Missouri. Convened in the City of St. Louis. Oct 12, 1846* (St. Louis: Keenle & Field, 1847), 53.

71 A registered physician in Platte City. Paxton, *Annals of Platte County*, 97.

Owing to the great distance and the infrequent departure of emigrant trains for the Northwest, it was several months before an opportunity was found to transmit the charter to the Brethren for whose benefit it had been ordered. In the latter part of December, 1847, Brother Pierre Barlow Cornwall was making up a party to come west, from St. Joseph, Missouri; and to his care Brother Spratt entrusted the charter. Brother Cornwall started from St. Joseph with a party of five persons, about the 1st of April, 1848, but on account of hostile demonstrations on the part of Indians, they were detained near Omaha for several days....[72]

It was a brave twenty seven year old Freemason, albeit completely unrelated to any of the brothers in Oregon, that ended up bringing the first Masonic charter to the West Coast.[73]

Pierre Barlow Cornwall:
The Man Destined to Carry the Charter

Pierre Barlow Cornwall was born just outside of Andes in Delaware County, New York, on November 23, 1821.[74] His grandfather, Stephen Cornwall, had emigrated to the American colonies from England in the mid 1700s. In the wildly exciting times of the American Revolution, Pierre's grandfather had a child, William Cornwall.

During this period, what was good for the country was also good for the entrepreneur as a man's patriotism and personal gain were intricately linked during the late 1700s. This generation was made up of:

pioneers, men and women of strong character, foresight, courage and capability. Their descendants had inherited these traits and the conditions and circumstances of their lives enhanced the qualities transmitted. Thus, by natural selection, inheritance and training, was created a people, the nucleus of a Republic, strong, resolute, progressive and essentially pio-

---

72 Hodson, Upton, Brown & Hedges, *Masonic History of the Northwest*, 266.

73 Bruce Cornwall, *Life Sketch of Pierre Barlow Cornwall* (San Francisco: A.M. Robertson, 1906), 7.

74 Cornwall, *Life Sketch of Pierre Barlow Cornwall*, 1.

P.B. Cornwall, Member of Mansfield Lodge № 35 of the Grand Lodge of Ohio.

neers; men and women fitted to meet hardships and conquer them, able to look forward and create whatever mighte be lacking in civilization, in government, and in science, that their country should take its place, pre-eminent, amongst the nations of the earth.[75]

Pierre Cornwall's father, William Cornwall, grew up in central New York while the Astorian venture was happening on the opposite side of the continent. Surely he and most citizens on the East Coast were impacted by the War of 1812 when the ports of New York City were blocked. It's doubtful that he got a proper education yet he was growing up in the first free country under the Presidencies of George Washington, John Adams and Thomas Jefferson. One can only imagine the hope that parents had for their children during this era. These were the conditions in which William Cornwall grew up. In 1820 he married Theodosia Cornwall and the two had their first child, Pierre, the following year.[76] Always going where there was work, William moved his family from Central New York to a small town of Westfield on the shores of Lake Erie. Here he built a log cabin and raised his family in pioneer fashion near a small village.[77]

As Pierre grew up, he attended school during the winter months and spent the remainder of the year "clearing the land and conquering the country" at his family's property.[78] Eventually the opportunity came for William to open a general merchandise store for incoming settlers. At the age of ten, Pierre started working at this store and learned the ways of business. By fifteen, he became restless in this tiny village so he bundled up what little things he had and jumped on steamer bound for Buffalo, New York.[79]

One can only imagine the thrill that Pierre felt while striking off on his own with nothing but his wits and a few personal belongings. Like Bros. Kit Carson and John Jacob Astor before him, young Pierre would live a very colorful life despite his humble beginnings. His first job in Buffalo was working as a deckhand on a steamship which also became his place of residence at this time.[80] Through "his earnest devotion to work,

75 Cornwall, *Life Sketch of Pierre Barlow Cornwall*, 3.
76 Cornwall, *Life Sketch of Pierre Barlow Cornwall*, 4.
77 Cornwall, *Life Sketch of Pierre Barlow Cornwall*, 5.
78 Cornwall, *Life Sketch of Pierre Barlow Cornwall*, 8.
79 Cornwall, *Life Sketch of Pierre Barlow Cornwall*, 9.
80 Cornwall, *Life Sketch of Pierre Barlow Cornwall*, 10.

his cheerful disposition and kindly attitude" he won many friends and before long he was working for a major company.[81]

It was likely through this employment that Pierre became connected with various gentlemen in Buffalo that invited him to join the "Buffalo Apprentices' Society." The idea behind this society was to improve the lives of poor young boys through mentorship.[82] It is no wonder that Pierre later became a Freemason. During this time period he also joined Mansfield Lodge № 35 of the Grand Lodge of Ohio.

At the age of eighteen, Pierre purchased "frontier commodities" and set off again this time into the Great Lakes to become a fur trader. Had it been a decade earlier, maybe he would have ended up in the Rocky Mountains working for the American Fur Company. But as the trade was waning due to a dwindling beaver population, Pierre's stint as a trapper was short-lived. After just a few seasons, he ended up throwing in the towel and returning to his family in New York.

In his old town, Pierre found new responsibilities when his father passed away suddenly in 1840. He was now the man of the family and in charge of his father's estate.[83] Pierre ended up taking over his father's general store and running it for several years until 1847 when, after a series of failed investments, he would be forced to sell the store. Young Pierre was now very much in debt and in need of a fresh start.

The Call of the Wild West: 1848

Hearing about Frémont's expeditions on the West Coast was exactly what young men like P. B. Cornwall needed to hear. It was the ultimate "grass is greener on the other side" phenomenon, just on a continental scale. Pierre probably obtained Fremont's newly-printed narrative from the expeditions which painted a picture of endless opportunity.

Pierre like many others at the time, was sold on the idea of rolling the dice and moving west.[84] In March of 1848, Pierre and his younger brother

81 Cornwall, *Life Sketch of Pierre Barlow Cornwall*, 11.

82 Cornwall, *Life Sketch of Pierre Barlow Cornwall*, 12.

83 Cornwall, *Life Sketch of Pierre Barlow Cornwall*, 13.

84 There are several reasons why Americans headed west. Besides the propaganda backed "Manifest Destiny" there was just a simple desire to improve their livelihoods. Regular disastrous flooding, economic depressions, and malaria were other major reasons people headed west. See James R. Gibson, *Farming the Frontier. The Agricultural Opening of the Oregon Country, 1786-1846* (University of Washington Press, 1985), 133.

Alfred Jacob Miller (1810–1874). *Prairie Scene: Mirage.*
Watercolor on paper, c. 1860. Walters Art Museum.

Arthur, then only sixteen, made their way for Missouri. Word had not reached the States yet about the discoveries of gold in California but soon Pierre would be swept into that frenzy.

The two brothers purchased all the necessary supplies including mules, guns,[85] clothing, and food in St. Joseph, Missouri. They also hired a guide by the name of Tom Fallon,[86] a Scotch-Irish trapper formerly employed by Hudson's Bay Company.[87] Fallon spoke French, English and Indian dialects fluently and was a priceless addition to the party.

To those preparing to cross the Oregon trail, it must have felt similar to what their grandparents experienced when getting on a ship and crossing the Atlantic for America. However, there was one major difference. These emigrants would be completely responsible for getting themselves to their

---

85 One of the most common ways to die or be significantly injured on the trail was due to a firearm accidentally going off or being carelessly shot in the direction of a person. These guns were purchased as insurance against hostile Indians but obviously not properly handled. See Franklin Langworthy, *Scenery of the Plains, Mountains and Mines* (Ogdensburgh, N.Y.: J.C. Sprague, 1855), 63.

86 Said to be a brother Mason as well. Whitsell, *One Hundred Years of Freemasonry in California*, 13.

87 Cornwall, *Life Sketch of Pierre Barlow Cornwall*, 16.

destination. Essentially, St. Joseph was like an English wharf where thousands of people arrived every year to pool their money and buy sailboats, supplies and travel books to get them safely across the Atlantic. What an incredible gamble it was for these emigrants to risk literally everything they had to reach the bountiful farmlands in Oregon.

Aside from the amazing grit required of these early pioneers, it was also necessary that they put down a lot of money just to get started on the trail. Covered wagons cost about seventy-five dollars apiece but the true expense was for mules.[88] These hardy animals were said to be the real heroes of the Oregon Trail and could cost up to one thousand dollars for a full wagon team.[89] All told, the estimated cost for transporting a family across the Oregon Trail was between $800 and $1,200—well over $25,000 when adjusted for inflation.[90]

Somehow during Pierre's preparations at St. Joseph he connected with brother James Spratt of Platte City Lodge. The specifics of how the two met is left to the reader's imagination as the original records of both Platte City and Multnomah Lodge were destroyed in fires. Regardless of how they met, brother James had found the perfect person to carry the first Masonic charter across the plains to Oregon City. It was April of 1848 when Cornwall set off from "St. Joe" under what had to be an absolutely electric atmosphere and every bit as exciting as a modern blockbuster movie.

> Each little party severed the ties which bound it to loved ones and friends, for they knew not how long it would be: abandoning home comforts…with firm resolve set their faces westward to reach a region whose location, advantages and possibilities were but little known. To exile themselves across such as wide and dangerous expanse called for a faith most sublime, a heroism sterling, and a spirit daring even to the verge of madness.[91]

Many were daily falling victims to this dreaded scourge (cholera[92]), while

---

88 Buck, *The Oregon Trail*, 72.

89 Buck, *The Oregon Trail*, 39.

90 Dorothy Johansen, *Empire of the Columbia: A History of the Pacific Northwest* (New York: Harper & Row, 1967).

91 H. George Himes, "Oregon Pioneer Association." *Oregon Native Son and Historical Magazine*, June 1899, 8.

92 "Cholera waited in the brackish streams and waterholes, left by one party, to be

John C. H. Grabill (1849–1903). *Freighting in the Black Hills.*
Photographic print, 1887. Library of Congress.

many others were becoming disheartened and were turning back to their homes. Everything here was bustle and wild confusion.[93]

A few days out from St. Joseph they arrived at the Council Bluffs of the Missouri River. Here they joined a larger group of an estimated five hundred emigrants bound for Oregon.[94] The eager emigrants were staged for proper conditions to advance across the plains. It was important to start out in mid-May in order to catch the grass at its tallest, thus ensuring the pack animals would be well fed through the journey.[95]

For the Cornwall trio, getting stuck behind a massive train of emigrants would not do. Instead, they opted to join a smaller train to get ahead of

passed on to the next group following across the plains. The route westward was marked with wooden crosses and stone cairns, the crosses often bearing only a name and 'cholera'. Nowhere could the disease have been more terrifying than on those trails, where men died without physicians, without ministers and without friends." Charles Rosenberg, *The Cholera Years: The United States in 1832, 1849 and 1866* (Chicago: University of Chicago Press, 1987), 118.

93 Kimball Webster, *The Gold Seekers of '49: A Personal Narrative of the Overland Trail and Adventures in California and Oregon from 1849 to 1854* (Manchester, N.H.: Standard Book Co., 1917), 35.

94 Cornwall, *Life Sketch of Pierre Barlow Cornwall*, 15.

95 Langworthy, *Scenery of the Plains*, 18.

Albert Bierstadt (1830–1902). *Campfire.*
Oil on Canvas, c. 1863. Mead Art Museum, Amherst, Massachusetts.

the giant "motley company" of wagons.[96]

> A man was seldom refused permission—if he asked for it—to join a
> train, since there was safety in numbers. The result was a gathering of
> strangers, many of whom were suspicious of their fellow travelers, and
> not without good reason.[97]

The group they ended up joining consisted of thirty wagons. In
charge of this wagon train were Bros. Orrin and Joseph Kellogg, a father
and son who were moving their whole family to Oregon.[98] The Kelloggs

96 Cornwall, *Life Sketch of Pierre Barlow Cornwall,* 15.

97 Vestal, Stanley. The Old Santa Fe Trail. University of Nebraska Press: 1939. 41

98 Orrin and Joseph Kellogg were father and son but Masonic brothers. The Masonic
    activities of Orrin Kellogg began in Murray Lodge Nº 17 United Ancient York Ma-
    sons under the Village of St. Andrews in His Majesties Province of Lower Canada.
    He applied for the degrees on October 4, 1814, was initiated on November 1, 1814,
    and was presumed to be passed and raised on December 13, 1814. On January 7, 1817
    he dimited from Murray Lodge and moved to New York State. (Frank Knoll, *How
    Masonry Came to Oregon,* 20). Joseph Kellogg petitioned Phoenix Lodge Nº 123 in
    Perrysburg, Ohio on January 18, 1847. He was entered and passed on June 28, 1847

were well outfitted for the trip with massive oxen to pull their wagons.[99] Bro. Orrin Kellogg was joined by his wife, his sons Joseph and Charles II and his two daughters who were accompanied by their husbands, Daniel and Sylvester Hathaway.

In the biography he wrote about his father, Bruce Cornwall noted the presence of the charter destined for Oregon City:

> My father had had intrusted to his care, for preservation and safe trans-mittal, a Masonic Charter…to Multnomah Lodge, № 84 of Oregon City. It was on parchment and securely enclosed in a tin cylinder. The Kelloggs, who were strong, able-bodied and minded men and Masons, formed a welcome addition to the little party….[100]

The group of emigrants made steady progress along the Platte River as they learned the temperaments of their animals and of each other. Gradually their thoughts about the past faded as they scanned the horizon for danger. Scattered all about the prairie were piles of buffalo bones bleaching in the sun from past Pawnee hunting parties.

This American Serengeti was characterized by remarklable bio- and geo-diversity. Some of the more interesting sights for passing wagon trains were vast prairie dog fields and huge mud pits created by wallowing buffalo. These buffalo wallows could be up to fifty feet across and generally filled with rain water or quicksand depending on the time of year. The quick sand could be a nightmare for any pack animals or wagons that were driven into it.[101] Yet along with these dangers, nature always provides man with means to survive. Peppered amongst a sea of rolling grassland was an unlimited supply of buffalo dung which proved to be an essential resource to these pioneers.[102]

After a month of slow yet steady progress, a man was seen coming at

---

and raised on August 9, 1847.

99 Kimball Harvey Hines, *An Illustrated History of the State of Oregon: Containing a History of Oregon from the Earliest Period of Its Discovery to the Present Time, Together with Glimpses of Its Auspicious Future; Illustrations and Full-page Portraits of Some of Its Eminent Men and Biographical Mention of Many of Its Pioneers and Prominent Citizens of To-day* (Chicago: Lewis Pub. Co., 1893), 1037.

100 Cornwall, *Life Sketch of Pierre Barlow Cornwall*, 16.

101 Stanley Vestal, *The Old Santa Fe Trail* (University of Nebraska Press, 1939), 76.

102 These "buffalo chips" were often used as fuel for camp fires due to the lack of trees and wood on the prairie.

Alfred Jacob Miller (1810–1874). *Indian Council.*
Watercolor on paper, c. 1858. The Walters Art Museum, Baltimore.

them in haste heading in the opposite direction. It was Joe Meek[103] who was on his way back to Washington, D.C. He told the Cornwalls about the horrible Whitman Massacre which had just occurred the previous fall, and that he was on his way to make an appeal for military support in the Oregon territory.

Indian Country: Captured by the Pawnees

Cornwall's first test on the trail would come as they made their way through Pawnee territory. One day they crested a hill and surprised a large encampment of Pawnee Indians. It is alleged that the emigrants were surrounded by the Pawnees and taken as prisoners.[104]

Emotions were tense among the Pawnees that evening. Apparently American emigrants had recently killed members of their tribe and revenge would be taken out on this unrelated party.

Fortunately the elders members of the tribe decided to release the prisoners the following day. Cornwall and company carried on rattled

103 A former mountain man who used to trap with Kit Carson. (*Santa Fe Book*, 180.)
104 Cornwall, *Life Sketch of Pierre Barlow Cornwall*, 18.

yet grateful to be alive. The following night they found rest near the banks of the Platte River and sixteen year old Arthur Cornwall kept watch through the night.

A few hours into his watch, Arthur set the alarm and all were awoken to the fact that a group of Pawnees were sneaking up on them. The riflemen of the wagon train were able to hold off the attackers long enough to allow their escape. Brother Cornwall was said to have taken an arrow just below the knee during this skirmish causing him a "serious wound."[105]

After a long retreat, the wary emigrants set up camp for the night filled with dread. The night passed without incident, but the following morning they spotted another Indian party approaching from the distance. As the group got closer, the Indians were recognized from their headdresses as Sioux rather than Pawnee. In fact, in this very group was Fallon's father in law. Imagine the relief they felt as they were able to release the clutch on their rifles and take in a full breath of fresh air.[106]

After a short exchange, the Sioux bolted off in search of the Pawnees who had been terrorizing them. It turned out the Sioux and Pawnee were bitter enemies and Cornwall's party was right in the middle of their feud. The Americans continued up the Platte River and were later joined by the same Sioux warriors. Everyone cheered when they reported a fierce battle with the Pawnees.[107] The following day under escort of these Sioux warriors, they reached the safety of Fort Laramie where they could rest in safety.[108]

After a few days spent at Fort Laramie they continued westward and passed the iconic Independence Rock—which, by this point in 1848, was already covered in engravings from passing emigrants. When John C. Frémont visited the rock in August of 1843, he noted that:

> Everywhere within six or eight feet of the ground, where the surface is sufficiently smooth, and in some places sixty or eighty feet above, the rock is inscribed with the names of travelers. Many a name famous in the history of this country, and some well known to science, are to be found among those of traders and travelers.... Some of these have been

---

105 Cornwall, *Life Sketch of Pierre Barlow Cornwall*, 21.
106 Cornwall, *Life Sketch of Pierre Barlow Cornwall*, 22.
107 Cornwall, *Life Sketch of Pierre Barlow Cornwall*, 23.
108 Located on the Platte River in modern day South Eastern Wyoming.

washed away by the rain, but the greater number are still visible.[109]

Thanks to the reports provided by Frémont's expedition, emigrants like Cornwall were able to find the South Pass which was like a gateway through the Rockies and marked the start of the western slope of the Continent. Gone were the days when people would have to get lost in this wilderness like Bro. Hunt had thirty-seven years before. Yet even though Bro. Cornwall was well aware of what lay ahead on the trail, nothing could have prepared him for the news that was awaiting him at the next major stop.

The California Gold Rush: January 24, 1848

It was the work of but a few weeks to bring almost the entire population of the territory together to pick up pieces of precious metal. The result has been, that in less than four months, a total revolution has been effected in the prospects and fate of Alta, California. Then, capital was in the hands of a few individuals engaged in trade and speculation; now labor has got the upper hand of capital, and the laboring men hold the great mass of wealth in the country—the gold.[110]

On the morning of January 24, 1848, two men were attempting to build a sawmill on the banks of the American River just east of Sacramento, California.[111] One was a Swiss entrepreneur named John Sutter; the other, James W. Marshall a carpenter who Sutter hired to build his mill.[112] On this fateful day the two men discovered something that would send shock waves out to the rest of the world. The discovery of a few flakes of gold at Sutter's mill would ignite the California gold rush and as a result, tilt a major part of the American population to the west coast.

This is the common history of what happened when gold was first discovered. In an alternate version, the discovery happened three years earlier when a man named Charles R. Bennett—while on Frémont's ex-

109 John C. Frémont, *Report of the Exploring Expedition to the Rocky Mountains in the Year 1842* (Washington, D.C.: Gales & Seaton, 1845), 57.

110 *The San Francisco Californian*, August 14, 1848.

111 Roughly halfway between the city of Sacramento and Lake Tahoe in the El Dorado National Forest.

112 J. Malcolm Rohrbough, *Days of Gold: The California Gold Rush and The American Nation* (Berkeley: University of California Press, 1997), 7.

Alfred Jacob Miller (1810–1874). *The Interior of Fort Laramie.*
Watercolor on paper, c. 1858. The Walters Art Museum, Baltimore.

pedition in 1845—saw gold in the same river as Marshall.[113] After briefly
settling down in Salem, Oregon, Bennett returned to the American River
in Alta California. According to some accounts, he was the one who initially showed the gold to Marshall.[114]

Cornwall Changes Course

By the summer of 1848, when the Cornwall party arrived at Fort Hall,[115] the
banks of the American River were already swarming with people panning for
gold. That summer, the first wave of the gold rush was composed of mostly
native Californios who worked by themselves or alongside their families.[116]

113 Member of Salem Lodge Nº 4 in Salem, Oregon.

114 Whitsell, *One Hundred Years of Freemasonry in California*, 55. Captain Charles Bennett's tombstone in Salem, Oregon states that it was he who found the first gold in
California. See Webster, *The Gold Seekers of '49*, 237.

115 Located on the Snake River in the south eastern corner of Idaho.

116 Rohrbough, *Days of Gold*, 9.

Still-perceptible wagon ruts from the mid-1800s at Iron Springs
along the Santa Fe Trail in Otero County, Colorado.

Then the next wave came followed by another. Each wave got bigger and bigger until "every male in central California who could move or be carried and…could jettison their present commitments, whether professional or personal"[117] headed straight for the gold. That frenzied excitement steadily spread out in every direction and eventually it reached Fort Hall.

In early August, Pierre B. Cornwall and his party of thirty wagons pulled in to the HBC post of Fort Hall where they caught the exciting news about gold being found in California.[118] It is anyones guess how that conversation went but the effect it had on Pierre Cornwall was obvious. He decided right then and there that he was going to head for the gold fields in California.

To hell with farming—panning for gold in California sounded much better than breaking his back plowing fields in Oregon. But what about the Masonic charter he was supposed to deliver to Oregon City?

117 Rohrbough, *Days of Gold*, 10.
118 The charter was subsequently delivered to Oregon City on September 11, 1848 from Fort Hall. If traveling an average rate of twenty-five miles per day which was to be expected on horseback, it would have taken around thirty days (or the date the charter arrived). "They made nearly twenty-five miles a day, and arrived at Milwaukee, Oregon, September 8, 1848."

Kellogg's trunk.
Courtesy of Brother Johnny J. Edwards, Grand Lodge of Oregon Museum.

Multnomah's Charter Changes Hands: August, 1848

For Cornwall, the opportunities in California were far more attractive than those he expected to find in Oregon, but not so for Orrin[119] and Joseph[120] Kellogg. The Kelloggs were also Freemasons themselves, and as such, Cornwall entrusted them with completing the mission of delivering the charter. While it may have been permissible to allow a trustworthy

119 As reported in *Oregon Native Son and Historical Magazine:* "Born: Sep. 4, 1790, Saint Albans, Franklin County, Vermont, USA. Died: Feb. 14, 1873. Portland, Multnomah County, Oregon, USA. His ancestors were of Revolutionary stock. Prior to Oregon, he lived in Canada, Lockport, N.Y. and Ohio before moving to St. Joseph, Mo. to prepare for his journey West. He took up a donation claim in Milwaukie, Oregon there building up one of the first fruit orchards in the area. Captain Kellogg was a man of great liberality, never stinting his hospitality to travelers or strangers, and as for his friends, they always found the latch string on the outside of his door, indicative of hearty welcome. All in all, Captain Orrin Kellogg was a man of robust character and sterling worth, one of that class of men whose energy, fairness and goodness are of the utmost value in the formation of a commonwealth, and make it pleasurable to live in after the ball has begun to roll." (Vol. 1, No. 2., June 1899, 111).

120 As reported in *Oregon Native Son and Historical Magazine:* "Born: June 24, 1812 in Canada. Lived most of live up until 1847 as a farmer in Ohio. Took up a claim like his father in Milwaukee, Oregon and became successful businessman and steamboat captain. He and brother Mason Lot Whitcomb built the first large steamboat in Oregon the "Lot Whitcomb." (Vol. 1, No. 2., June 1899, 112).

individual who was not connected to the Craft to deliver the charter, the fact that the Kelloggs were Freemasons made their selection more appropriate, and perhaps more providential. The beauty of the story lies in the unbroken chain of masons who were able to complete the mission from beginning to end.

Congress creates the Territory of Oregon: August 14, 1848

Spurred on by the deaths of Dr. Marcus Whitman, his wife, and eleven others at their mission in Walla Walla, Washington, the Federal Government established the Territorial Government of Oregon.[121] With this, Bro. Polk checks off one item from his Presidential to do list. For the Kelloggs, this meant they were now delivering a Masonic charter to the American Territory of Oregon rather than the jointly-occupied "Oregon Country."

Onward to Oregon Territory: September, 1848

The Cornwalls split off from the Oregon Trail and started down the California trail with a new group of forty-five emigrants. The Kelloggs meanwhile, continued on the Oregon Trail for the final stretch through modern day Idaho and Oregon. They would effortlessly pass through the same landscape in southern Idaho where brother Hunt had gotten lost and nearly starved to death three decades earlier.

Needless to say, it was a much more pleasant experience for the Kelloggs to follow wagon ruts and camp safely at trading forts along the way. From Fort Hall, they safely made it to the Willamette Valley without any problems.[122] After staking a claim at a nearby town called Milwaukie,[123] the Kelloggs fulfilled the duty of delivering the charter to Bro. Joseph Hull in Oregon City. It was September 11, 1848, and the Freemasons in Oregon City had been waiting now for two years, seven months, and six days. Not willing to waste any more time, Bro. Hull called together a meeting that very day and Multnomah Lodge No 84 became active.[124] It was the first

121 Walt Crowley, "Congress creates Territory of Oregon on August 14, 1848." (2003). *http://www.historylink.org/File/5245.*

122 The Whitman Massacre had just occurred the previous fall.

123 Brother Lot Whitcomb first settled in this town as a rival and midpoint between Portland and Oregon City in 1847. See Hines, *An Illustrated History of the State of Oregon*, 1094.

124 Hodson, Upton, Brown & Hedges, *Masonic History of the Northwest*, 268.

chartered Masonic lodge to meet on the west coast of the continent—by far the most remote American lodge in existence.

Bro. William P. Dougherty, one of the original signers of the petition, owned a two-story log building which was consecrated as the meeting place. Perhaps warmed by a small wooden stove and illuminated by the flickering glow of oil lamps, the brethren assembled for the first meeting of Multnomah Lodge.

Bro. Berryman Jennings[125] acted as the installing officer for the following positions:

Joseph Hull: Worshipful Master
Orrin Kellogg: Senior Warden
Fendal Cason: Junior Warden
Joseph Kellogg: Treasurer
Joel Palmer: Secretary[126]
Lot Whitcomb: Senior Deacon[127]

125 Berryman Jennings' career is to be found in the records of five different states-Kentucky, Illinois, Iowa, California and Oregon. He was born in Kentucky in 1807, moved to Illinois, and in 1830 in Iowa, became the first school teacher in the first schoolhouse north of the Missouri, and between the Mississippi River and the Pacific Ocean. Jennings was raised in Des Moines Lodge Nº 1, Burlington, Iowa, in 1845, and demitted to become a member of Multnomah Lodge of Oregon City, Oregon when he moved West. He first settled in Oregon City, but, for a short period, lived in California. He became Senior Warden of New Jersey Lodge U.D., at Sacramento, December 4, 1849. In April, 1850, he was a member of the convention that organized the Grand Lodge of California, and was elected the first Grand Treasurer of the Grand Lodge of California. But he resigned on returning to Oregon shortly thereafter. He affiliated with Multnomah Lodge Nº 84 (now Nº 1), and remained a member until his death. Also, he helped establish Willamette Lodge Nº 2 in Portland, and was a member of the convention called to form the Grand Lodge of Oregon. He became Oregon's first Grand Master, serving two years. In Sacramento, California, New Jersey Lodge was named after Jennings, being called at first Berryman Lodge Nº 4 and later renamed Jennings Lodge Nº 4. (Leon Whitsell, *One Hundred Years of Freemasonry in California*, 220-21.)

126 Palmer had returned to Oregon City in the Fall of 1847 with his wife Sarah and their five children. See Terence O'Donnell, *An Arrow in the Earth. General Palmer and the Indians of Oregon*, (1991), 56. Also see Hubert Howe Bancroft, *The History of Oregon, 1886-1888* (San Francisco History Co., 1886-88), 626.

127 Published Democratic newspaper at Milwaukee, Oregon called the Western Star, of which John Orvis Waterman was editor. (*History of the Pacific Northwest-Oregon and Washington*, Volume 1 (1889), North Pacific History Company of Portland Oregon, 319). Built a steamboat called "Lot Whitcomb" captained by Brother John C. Ainsworth to run the Columbia and Willamette Rivers (*History of the Pacific Northwest-Oregon*

Berryman Jennings: Junior Deacon

J. H. Bosworth: Tyler

It is uncertain how many other brothers were in attendance during that first meeting due to all of the original documents being destroyed by a fire in 1857. According to Hodson, there were three candidates that were entered, passed, and raised to the sublime degree of Mater Mason during this first meeting.[128] They were Christopher Taylor,[129] Amos L. Lovejoy,[130] and Albert E. Wilson. This marathon communication was said to lasted for a total of sixteen hours before it closed in the early morning hours of the following day.[131]

The Multnomah Brothers Drop Everything and Leave for California: Mid September 1848

One of the most shocking developments of Multnomah Lodge is also a testament to the power of that precious metal being found in the rivers of central California. Before Multnomah Lodge met for its first meeting, William Dougherty, whose name was printed on the charter, had already departed for California. Within a day or two after the first lodge meeting, Joseph Hull[132] who had been obligated to lead his brethren for the ensuing

and Washington [North Pacific History Company of Portland Oregon, 1889], 320).

128 John Milton Hodson, Past Grand Master of the Grand Lodge of Oregon and "one of the most prominent members of the Masonic fraternity on the Pacific coast, founder and ex-editor of the Eugene Register, ex-deputy collector of customs for the Port of Portland and ex-secretary of the Irwin-Hodson Company. While Mr. Hodson was prominent in business and industrial affairs of Portland and the state, it was through his Masonic connections that he became best known. Through his work in that fraternity he became acquainted, by correspondence, with the jurisdictions in all parts of the world. He was probably the best informed man in the history of Masonry on the Pacific coast. The later years of his life were devoted almost entirely to his work for the organization which he loved." *The Oregonian*, Oct. 10, 1910, 8.

129 Arrived in Oregon City in 1847 with Joel Palmer's wagon train. See Bancroft, *The History of Oregon*, 626.

130 Amos Lovejoy went on to become a prominent member of the territory. He had arrived in the first large wagon party of 1842 with Dr. Elijah White.

131 Hodson, Upton, Brown & Hodges, *Masonic History of the Northwest*, 268.

132 In September of 1891, Worshipful Brother Hull returned from California (not for the first time) to Multnomah Lodge No. 1 in Oregon City where he was received with all the honors. Brother Joseph Kellogg was present at this reception. See A. Edwin Sherman, *Fifty Years of Masonry in California* (San Francisco: G. Spaulding, 1898),

Alfred Jacob Miller (1810–1874). *Landing the Charettes.* c. 1858.
Pencil on paper, The Walters Art Museum, Baltimore.

year as Worshipful Master, also left for California.[133] Brother Hull—like many able bodied men in Oregon Territory—ventured south with hopes of striking it rich.[134]

It is not known exactly how many people left Oregon for California during this frenzied time, but it is likely that Hull joined a relatively small group of other men. They would have traveled on horseback following the newly developed Applegate Trail to southern Oregon.[135]

1:47; Asa Merrill Fairfield, *Fairfield's Pioneer History of Lassen County California* (San Francisco: H.S. Crocker, 1916), 311

133 Hodson, Upton, Brown & Hedges, *Masonic History of the Northwest*, 268.

134 $30,000 to $50,000 was being dug up daily during the initial months of the gold rush. These first miners were simply whoever was in the immediate area. People of every background dropped their responsibilities and went to look for gold. See Fremont, *Oregon and California*, 432.

135 Before it was called the Applegate Trail, the route was used by Indians to trade with each other. See Jeff Zucker, Jay Forest Penniman, Kay Hummel, Bob Høgfoss, & Faun Rae Hosey, *Oregon Indians: Culture, History and Current Affairs* (Portland: Oregon Historical Society Press, 1987), 42. Later it became a closely guarded secret of the Hudson's Bay Company as it was used by HBC trappers to reach California. (Claude W. Nichols, *The South Road: Its Development and Significance*, 36) As the fur trade died down, the route was used to drive livestock from the Bay Area in California to Fort Vancouver and the Willamette Valley (Parrish, Philip H. Before the covered wagon. Binfords & Mort, 1956. 128) It got its name in June of 1846 when a

P.B. Cornwall Building, 1013 Second Street, Sacramento, California.
Library of Congress.

~~After passing through the undeveloped wilderness of southern~~
Oregon, they eventually came to the head of the Pit River in northern
California. Here they overtook a wagon train being led by a man named
Peter Lassen, who—it turns out—was leading a party of twelve wagons
back from Missouri to settle on his ranch.[136]

As for Pierre Cornwall, by this point he had already done his time
looking for gold on the American River and had moved into the lucrative
trade of "mining the miners."[137] His experience in running his father's
store back in New York proved valuable as he now ran a store in a historic

group of fifteen Oregon settlers led by Jesse Applegate set out to find a wagon road
to the Oregon settlements by way of a southern route. Mr. Applegate was successful
largely because of a Hudson Bay Co map he was given by Peter Ogden, then Chief
Factor of Fort Vancouver (Nichols, *The South Road*, 72). The result of this expedition
was the opening of the "Applegate Trail" which connected Willamette Valley to the
California Trail (The California Trail connected Fort Hall to Sacramento).

136 A. Edwin Sherman, *Fifty Years of Masonry in California* (San Francisco: G. Spaulding,
1898), 1:47; Asa Merrill Fairfield, *Fairfield's Pioneer History of Lassen County California*
(San Francisco: H.S. Crocker, 1916), 3.

137 Pierre B. Cornwall ran a general merchandise store in Drytown, California. "It was
a bustling inflated world of commerce in California then. Cornwall, *Life Sketch of
Pierre Barlow Cornwall*, 28.

Gold Miners, El Dorado, California. c. 1848. Library of Congress.

mining camp near the American River.

Cornwall would go on to serve on the state of California's first constitutional convention[138] in January 1849,[139] get elected to the first city council of Sacramento in July,[140] and was elected to the State Legislature in December.[141] By April of 1850, he sold his mercantile business and became quite wealthy.[142] Later, in the 1860s, he became President of the board of

---

138 President of convention: Brother Robert Semple, Treasurer of Benicia Lodge N° 5. See Whitsell, *One Hundred Years of Freemasonry in California*, 63. Abel Stearns. Elisha Oscar Crosby, Member of San Jose Lodge N° 10. See Whitsell, *One Hundred Years of Freemasonry in California*, 75. Lansford Warren Hastings, Member of Tehama Lodge N° 3, Whitsell, *One Hundred Years of Freemasonry in California*, 77. James McHall Jones, See Member of St. James Lodge N° 47 of Baton Rouge, Louisiana. See Whitsell, *One Hundred Years of Freemasonry in California*, 83. Myron Norton, See Member of California Lodge N° 1. Rodman M. Price, See Governor of New Jersey. Member of Union Lodge No 11. New Jersey. See Whitsell, *One Hundred Years of Freemasonry in California*, 81.

139 Cornwall, *Life Sketch of Pierre Barlow Cornwall*, 31.

140 Cornwall, *Life Sketch of Pierre Barlow Cornwall*, 33.

141 Cornwall, *Life Sketch of Pierre Barlow Cornwall*, 38.

142 Cornwall, *Life Sketch of Pierre Barlow Cornwall*, 45.

The city of Sacramento, California, drawn from the foot of J Street by G.V. Cooper on December 20, 1849. Library of Congress, Prints and Photographs Division.

trustees for the Black Diamond Coal Company,[143] which operated out of San Francisco and had mines in Bellingham, Washington.[144]

In the late 1870s, Cornwall owned two steamships, the *California* and the *Great Republic* which ran back and forth between San Francisco and Portland.[145] Tragically, the latter added itself to the wreckage already littering the mouth of the Columbia when it crashed in 1878, claiming the lives of fourteen crewmen. With that, the story of the Wild West comes full circle. Just three generations after Bro. Astor chartered the *Tonquin* to sail from New York City to the Columbia River in the fur trade, Bro. Cornwall had steam powered ships moving people and goods from the same river to San Francisco.

One hundred and sixty years later, Bellingham, Washington honors Pierre Cornwall's legacy with Cornwall Avenue and Cornwall Park, the latter of which includes a Masonic[146] monument dedicated to him. In the

143 The Black Diamond Coal Company operated a mine in Bellingham Bay which brought a boost to the tiny town.

144 Cornwall, *Life Sketch of Pierre Barlow Cornwall*, 59.

145 Cornwall, *Life Sketch of Pierre Barlow Cornwall*, 62.

146 In 1949, exactly one hundred years after the gold rush, a Masonic Lodge was chartered

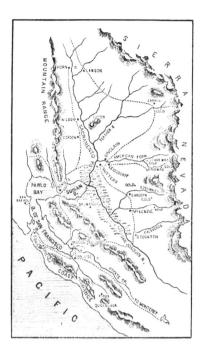

Map showing the location of Lassen's ranch (shown as Lawson). From Frémont's *Report of the Exploring Expedition to the Rocky Mountains in the Year 1842.*

historic district of downtown Sacramento, on the actual site of his general store, shoppers can visit the P.B. Cornwall Building.

Brother Peter Lassen
and California's First Masonic Charter: 1848

Brother Lassen[147] was born in Copenhagen, Denmark, in 1800 and was one of the true old world pioneers of the West. In 1839, he joined a wagon party in Missouri and traveled to Oregon City where he stayed for a year before jumping on a ship bound for California.[148] There he built California's first sawmill near Santa Cruz before obtaining a massive 22,000 acre ranch east

---

in Bellingham under the name "Pierre B Cornwall Lodge Nº 289." This Lodge later consolidated with Bellingham Bay Lodge Nº 44 in 2001. Bellingham Bay Lodge is the author's Mother Lodge.

147 He was named as the Junior Warden on the dispensation for Western Star Lodge Nº 98 under the Grand Lodge of Missouri.

148 The ship was called the *Lausanne*. See Whitsell, *One Hundred Years of Freemasonry in California*, 66.

of modern day Redding, California.[149] On this ranch Lassen incidentally hosted Frémont and his men while they surveyed the surrounding area in the Spring of 1846.[150]

In 1847, Lassen returned to Missouri in an effort to attract and bring back settlers to a portion of his land he had platted for development.[151] In the process of doing so, Lassen brought back a dozen wagons. One of these wagons was driven by Reverend Saschel Woods[152] who had in his possession a freshly printed Masonic charter for Western Star Lodge N° 98 under the Grand Lodge of Missouri.[153]

As the first Masonic charter to arrive in California made its way down the dusty wagon road, it is said to have literally crossed paths with Brother Hull's group while they were on their way down from Oregon City—a seemingly impossible coincidence that was not known to either group at the time.[154]

Being that Lassen was the only one familiar with the region, Brother Hull joined Lassen's wagon train until they reached the safety of Lassen's Ranch. Here, the Oregonians continued on for the gold fields while Brother Lassen opened a trading fort with another Freemason, Brother Isidore Meyerwitz.[155]

149 Lassen National Forest, Lassen Volcanic National Park, Lassen Peak and Lassen County all bear Peter Lassen's name for his development of the country. Additionally, Lassen Lodge N° 149 under the Grand Lodge of California bears his name.

150 John C. Frémont & H. William Emory, *Notes of Travel in California; Comprising the Prominent Geographical, Agricultural, Geological, and Mineralogical features of the country; also The Route from Fort Leavenworth, in Missouri, to San Diego, in California, including parts of the Arkansas, Del Norte, and Gila Rivers* (New York: D. Appleton & Co., 1849), 17.

151 Named after Thomas Hart Benton.

152 Previously a member of Wakanda Lodge N° 52 in Carrollton, Missouri. See Sherman, *Fifty Years of Masonry in California*, 1:65.

153 Petition signers were Samuel Woods, Lucian E. Stewart, Lorren, John Winters, Elisha Brown, P.J. Davis, D.H. Plemmens, Master Masons which was presented to the Grand Lodge of Missouri on Saturday, May 6, 1848. From the *Proceedings of the Grand Lodge of Missouri, convened in the city of St. Louis, May 1, 1848*, 25–26.

154 Sherman, *Fifty Years of Masonry in California*, 1:47.

155 A member of California N° 1. Sherman, *Fifty Years of Masonry in California*, 1:47.

Western Star Lodge No. 98: California's First Lodge

The first chartered Lodge in the Golden State was Western Star № 98. It began its labor on October 30, 1849, at Benton City on Lassen's ranch. Even though this was certainly the first Lodge to meet in California, it was mistakenly given the № 2 title when the Grand Lodge of California was formed in April of 1850. Within a year, the fallout from the gold rush caused Benton City to be largely abandoned and Western Star Lodge № 2 under the Grand Lodge of California was moved to the nearby town of Shasta, where it still meets today.[156]

Western Star Lodge № 2 continued to flourish until a fire in 1853 destroyed its hall and all of its records.

> On December 27, 1854, Saint John's Day, the Lodge was moved in Grand Procession to its new meeting place, a new brick building on Main Street. This building, referred to in 1854 as "Norton & Tucker's fireproof brick building" consisted of a basement, first and second floor. The second floor was purchased by the Lodge as its meeting place and from Saint John's Day of 1854 to the present, it has served as Western Star's Lodge room. In the late 1850s. The Lodge was able to purchase the remainder of the building. The first floor then became the banquet hall; and the basement continued for many years to be a storeroom.[157]

The End of the Old Wild West: 1850

The changes in California over a few short months were those characteristically associated with a plague or war…three quarters of the houses in San Francisco had been abandoned: every blacksmith, carpenter, and lawyer in the town had left for the mines; large numbers had deserted from the army in both San Francisco and Sonoma; crews had abandoned ships as soon as they anchored in San Francisco Bay; brickyards, sawmills, and ranches had been shut down by the absence of labor; the alcaldes of San Francisco and Sonoma had left to join the Gold Rush; newspapers had suspended publication for want of workingmen. The result was a "total revolution" in society and its economic relations.

---

156 Sherman, *Fifty Years of Masonry in California*, 1:100.

157 "A History of Western Star Lodge № 2." Western Star Lodge № 2, f & am. August 22, 2015. Accessed May 16, 2017. *http://westernstarlodge.org/about/a-history-of-western-star-lodge-2*.

Detail of *Shasta, Shasta County, California*. Drawn by Kuchel & Dresel.
Lithograph, hand colored, c. 1856. Library of Congress.

Before 1848, wealth in California generally had been defined by large landed estates with comfortable houses, by trade in hides and tallow through the small seaports, or by a particular trade or skill that was in demand. Gold rapidly transformed upper California into a gold-based cash economy. Goods and services were quoted in ounces of gold dust-visits to the doctor or lawyer were generally one ounce....

The accumulation of fortunes in the form of gold by substantial numbers of people established new ways of thinking about wealth. In this new world, gold was not slowly acquired over generations by hard work and influence. Instead, it lay on all sides, it was easily obtained and easily spent, and it seemed infinitely replenishable.[158]

By the Fall of 1848, conditions in California would truly start to transform into the "Wild West" we know from Hollywood. Expectant capitalists starting streaming in from all directions including those on the Hawaiian Islands, Mexico, Chile, and as far away as Australia. By Spring of 1849, the first ships started to arrive from the eastern States.[159] Later in the year, twenty five thousand emigrants came across the Oregon Trail.[160] It is said that when California found gold, the world found California.

158 Rohrbough, *Days of Gold*, 16-18.
159 Rohrbough, *Days of Gold*, 19.
160 Buck, *The Oregon Trail*, 118.

Along with the thousands of 49ers, a total of fifteen Masonic charters would also come to California during this frenzied time.[161] Perhaps these lodges brought the same value to men's lives in 1849 as they do today. Perhaps one could answer that question by talking to the brothers of Multnomah Lodge Nº 1 in Portland, Oregon or Western Star Lodge Nº 2 in Shasta, California. Both lodges still meet regularly today, thanks to an unbroken chain of brothers that continue to show up month after month, year after year, bringing value to this ancient fraternity.

161 Some of the lodges that were formed during this year still operate to this day. The oldest charter in California is still extant today at Western Star Lodge in Shasta, California. See Sherman, *Fifty Years of Masonry in California*, 1:86. And *http://www.redding.com/lifestyle/travelin-in-time-oldest-masonic-lodge-in-the-state-ep-376250466-355078321.html*.

Conclusion

Since the first Masonic Lodge opened on the West Coast, tens of thousands of men have entered the fraternity and bettered themselves through the ancient teachings found in the Craft. In this vast pool of masons, it is clear that some had a major influence on the world. The fact that these unique men were Masons does not suggest that Freemasonry endowed them with special powers. It is more likely that these men already possessed incredible minds to begin with which Freemasonry merely enhanced and refined.

A man's desire to join Freemasonry is said to arise from within his heart. Of the many reasons a man may petition a Lodge, inspiration is surely one of the most noble and indeed why this book was written. It should be inspiring for anyone, mason or non-mason alike to read about the tremendous work that the average man in the 19th century put into making a living. The fact that some of these men chose to divide their time and energy into various social and philanthropic enterprises, Freemasonry often just being one of many, is almost super human. Thus it is wise to study the past not only to learn from it but also to be inspired by it.

The common saying today that men are just too busy to be involved in Freemasonry or other social ventures is an insult to the masons of the past. If any value was to be found in Freemasonry by the accomplished men of antiquity, then surely there is value to be found in it today.

The intention in writing *Freemasonry in the Wild West* was not to simply write another biographical study about famous Freemasons of the past. Rather, its true intention is to inspire people (more particularly Freemasons) that we have inherited a world built not only by the hand of Deity but through the incredible labor of human beings. There is no doubt the world was built for us to enjoy but that doesn't mean we get to sit back in refreshment and avoid contributing to its improvement.

According to one writer, Freemasonry teaches "not only the necessity, but the nobility, of labor." We don't even need to look past our own lives to see where our labor is needed. Once our own lives are put in order, we can then contribute to our Lodge, our community, and our Country.

The sand in the hourglass is running out for all of us. When the day inevitably comes that we are called from labor, what will we leave behind? Every Freemason is given the same teachings in the three degrees but it is ultimately up to the individual to decide what he does with these teachings.

The impressive work of our brothers in the past will forever deserve our admiration and respect. We must admonish ourselves that the only way to truly honor their work is to continue building on it and improve it. For too many years the Craft has been at refreshment. The time has never been more urgent for Master Masons to draw up plans on the trestle board and continue the Great Work.

West Coast Freemasonry Statistics as of 2017

Total Masons in California: 52,096
Total population of California: 39,144,818

Total Masons in Oregon: 7,947
Total population of Oregon: 4,028,977

Total Masons in Washington: 13,392
Total population of Washington: 7,170,351

Total Masons in America: 1,161,253

Acknowledgments

The work you now hold in your hands would have never been put together if it weren't for a group of people who rallied behind it. First and foremost, Plumbstone Books is the vehicle that drove the book to completion. If not for Plumbstone's interest, I may have never had the confidence to write the first manuscript (or the second or third).

Instead of a three-month summer project, the book matured and developed over the course of three years into something far bigger and better than what I had originally intended it to be. To that, I owe my editor, Shawn Eyer, all the credit for mentoring me through the process of writing a book.

Outside of the book itself, there are many people I want to thank for contributing financially. My biggest contributor was Washington Masonic Charities, which provided a generous grant to get the book into the initial stages of publication. Ken Gibson, director of WMC, was essential in making that grant happen.

After the grant, all financial contributions came from individual people who faithfully donated $50 in exchange for a copy of the book when released. Incredibly, one hundred people subscribed to this and I thank each and every one for believing in me and supporting this work.

I thank Freemasonry as an institution for teaching me how to live a better and more useful life. I am especially grateful to my mentor, W. Bro. Ken Gass, for taking the time to coach me through the three degrees and to impress upon me the value to be found in Freemasonry.

Finally, I have to thank my family. I thank my parents, Tim and Mel, for always believing in me and encouraging me that I can do anything. I thank them for loving me unconditionally and raising me to be an independent human being. I thank my brother and sister, Dan and Amy, for loving me when I didn't love myself and as a result, helping me become the man I am today. Lastly, I thank my dear wife Carrie. Everything is possible with you by my side. Thank you for teaching me how to laugh, to love, and to be.

Image Credits

Boston Atheneum, 111.

Bill Brigs, 89, 111, 123, 139, 147.

Buffalo Bill Center of the West, Cody, Wyoming, 130.

Butler Institute of American Art, 156–57.

Colby College Museum of Art, 31.

The Architect of the Capitol, xii.

Gilcrease Museum, 48.

Grand Lodge of Oregon Museum, 192

Jim Gumm, 139.

Harvard Art Museums, 137.

Frank J. Haynes, Library of Congress, 37.

Carol M. Highsmith, Library of Congress, 190.

A. Hornung, Adobe Stock, 144.

Jay, Abode Stock, 44.

Scott Johnson, 19

Joslyn Art Museum, 30, 123, 166, 169, 185

Kreulen, Adobe Stock, 42.

Library of Congress, 7, 14, 20, 22, 27, 86, 106, 107, 110, 114, 126, 132, 133, 140, 141, 163, 171, 176, 183, 191, 196, 197, 202.

Library of Congress, 204–5. Frank Marryat (1826–1855). San Francisco / S.F. Marryat, delt. Chromolithograph.

Mead Art Museum, 184

Mark Myers, 61, 68, 58–59.

Metropolitan Museum of Art, 98–99.

The Miriam and Ira D. Wallach Division of Art, 198.

Missouri History Museum, 175.

Montreal Museum of Fine Arts, 50.

The Museum of Fine Arts, 84.

National Archives and Records Administration, 55, 77.

National Gallery of Canada, 54.

Oregon Historical Society, 121.

Seattle Art Museum, 72–73.

B. G. Smith, Adobe Stock, 64.

St. Louis Art Museum, 143.

State Archive of the Russian Navy, 88.

Toronto Public Library, 14.

Tryfonov, Adobe Stock, 5.

Tyler Olson, Adobe Stock, 35.

University of Michigan Museum of Art, 51.

The Walters Art Museum, 28, 41, 118, 135, 181, 186, 189, 195.

Washington Historical Society, cover, 159.

Wikiart, 30, 31.

Wikimedia Commons, 11, 13, 88.

Krzysztof Wiktor, Adobe Stock, 117.

Wirepec, Adobe Stock, 38.

Wollertz, Adobe Stock, 32.

David Wright, 104.

Yale University, 167

Kyle Grafstrom was made a Mason at Bellingham Bay Lodge № 44 in Bellingham, Washington, while attending Western Washington University, where he earned a Bachelor of Applied Science degree in Cultural Anthropology. He is the 2017–2018 Worshipful Master of Verity Lodge № 59 in Kent, Washington.

Also from Plumbstone

The Way of the Craftsman:
A Search for the Spiritual Essence of Craft Freemasonry
W. Kirk MacNulty

Contemplating Craft Freemasonry:
Working the Way of the Craftsman
W. Kirk MacNulty

Exploring Early Grand Lodge Freemasonry:
Studies in Honor of the Tricentennial of the Establishment
of the Grand Lodge of England
Edited by Christopher B. Murphy *&* Shawn Eyer

The Meaning of Masonry
Walter Leslie Wilmshurst

The Masonic Initiation
Walter Leslie Wilmshurst

Sing the Art Divine:
A Traditional Masonic Songster
Nathan St. Pierre *&* Shawn Eyer

Ahiman: A Review of Masonic Culture & Tradition
Edited by Shawn Eyer

Masonic Perspectives:
The Thoughts of a Grand Secretary
Thomas W. Jackson

The Higher Spiritualization of Freemasonry
Karl Christian Friedrich Krause

CPSIA information can be obtained
at www.ICGtesting.com
Printed in the USA
LVHW07n2020100618
580262LV00001B/1/P

* 9 7 8 1 6 0 3 0 2 0 2 6 8 *